Becoming Lisa

Becoming Lisa

Lisa Kelly

Copyright © 2018 Lisa Kelly

The moral right of the author has been asserted.

Apart from any fair dealing for the purposes of research or private study, or criticism or review, as permitted under the Copyright, Designs and Patents Act 1988, this publication may only be reproduced, stored or transmitted, in any form or by any means, with the prior permission in writing of the publishers, or in the case of reprographic reproduction in accordance with the terms of licences issued by the Copyright Licensing Agency. Enquiries concerning reproduction outside those terms should be sent to the publishers.

Matador
9 Priory Business Park,
Wistow Road, Kibworth Beauchamp,
Leicestershire. LE8 0RX
Tel: 0116 279 2299
Email: books@troubador.co.uk
Web: www.troubador.co.uk/matador
Twitter: @matadorbooks

ISBN 978 1789013 856

British Library Cataloguing in Publication Data.
A catalogue record for this book is available from the British Library.

Printed and bound by CPI Group (UK) Ltd, Croydon, CR0 4YY
Typeset in 11pt Minion Pro by Troubador Publishing Ltd, Leicester, UK

Matador is an imprint of Troubador Publishing Ltd

MIX
Paper from
responsible sources
FSC® C013604

Preface

I was born in late December 1968 and named after the Irish comedian Dave Allan; my story takes you through my childhood torment into adulthood and my admittance to myself that I was not a Dave, not a male, but a female. A female who had the external workings of a male. I will describe my journey from that self-admittance to becoming Lisa, the woman I am today, the struggles I had to overcome and the hoops I had to jump through to get there.

There were lots of ups and downs, a roller coaster ride to reach where I am now, from feeling suicidal to feeling invincible, from suffering at the hands of bullies to watching karma come back to bite them hard. I also tell of my projects and how they helped to keep me going during the times when I could not see light at the end of the tunnel, my involvement in charity work through to public speaking.

A common misconception is that a transgender person is following a fantasy; another is that transgender people are gay men dressing as women. You'll see from my own story that no transgender person would follow a fantasy that involves a lot of pain, unless of course they are a masochist, but even then, only a very tiny percentage of fantasy-followers will go as far as permanent hair removal, let alone surgery. Nobody chooses to be transgender.

A common belief is that transgender people are gay men. There are nearly as many female-to-male transgender people as there are male-to-female. Sexual orientation also varies just like cis-gender people, cis-gender being people who identify as the same as their birth gender.

Of all transgender people, a staggering 84% think about ending their life at some stage; of those, 48% actually attempt to take their own life.

My hope with this book is that it will show fellow transgender people that life does get better, it is worth hanging in there and clinging on. I also hope that non-transgender people reading this book will gain a better knowledge about some of the things transgender people face day to day, a greater understanding of what makes someone change their gender. It really can be a matter of life or death in some cases.

In my autobiography of how I became Lisa, I have changed the names of everyone to protect their identity. The only real names used are my own, and celebrities Stephanie Hirst, DJ; occasional television presenter David Hoyle, a gay icon and anti-drag queen television star; and Tanya Rabbe-Webber, a renowned disabled artist, all of whom I consider to be good friends.

One

My childhood and how it shaped my future.

From a very early age I knew I was different to the other boys on my estate. I grew up in the 1970s, in a small town called Tadcaster, and the only games the boys played in those days seemed to be football and cricket. Formula 1 racing was not the big business that it is today; you only have to look at how many 'boy racers' there are today compared to the 1970s. Rugby, too, was still a minority sport, given very little TV coverage.

Now don't get me wrong, I learned from a very early age to try my best at these sports; in those days, if you were rubbish at sport, you got bullied. I didn't quite excel at football or cricket, but I did make it into the school team.

I got bullied for being different; making the school team, I hoped I wouldn't get bullied, or at least I would be bullied far less often. I knew I was different to the other boys, but I didn't know in what way. I knew I wanted to play with the girls and join in with them, but I didn't know why. I thought that maybe I was really a girl.

I did find solace in one sport that I could do on my own: fishing. It meant I could get away from people and I spent many days on my own fishing, and whilst I was enjoying trying to catch fish, I was away from the bullies.

Why was I bullied? As I mentioned, I was different to the other boys. I wasn't foreign or a person of colour, or anything like that, but I had long curly, wavy hair whereas in the 70s most boys had crew cuts, probably a grade two or three with clippers in today's terminology. I had a very skinny, almost girly, body, no sign of any muscle or indeed of any future muscle to come. I had a higher-pitched voice than the other boys, and all this in junior school just led to verbal bullying and to a much lesser extent physical bullying.

Sometimes I did get to play rounders for a short time before the boys crowded round and started the name-calling. I was being called things like 'poofter' and 'faggot', but I had no idea what they meant. Teachers put it down to just playground banter; that banter shaped me into a shy, timid boy, lacking in confidence.

I couldn't help feeling that I should be with the girls, but I didn't know why I had those feelings at that age. Back then there was no internet and the term 'transgender' was unheard of, but it just did not seem to sit right, that I was grouped with the boys and not with the girls. That era was soon after the UK partially decriminalised homosexuality; it had been ushered in quietly in 1967 and many people were still unaware of the legislation.

Let me go a little into life with my parents. Around the time I started junior school, my mother was becoming more independent. She started doing Women's Royal Voluntary Service work and joined the town council. Both of these often kept her away from home at crucial times of the day, the times when parents would normally be bonding and playing with their children.

My father worked shifts at the brewery; Tadcaster was a brewery town with three breweries, so when he worked afternoons I wouldn't see him at all. Mornings and night shifts, all I saw of my dad was a few hours at teatime, when we would eat tea and he would have the early evening news on the television, followed by a chat show or light entertainment show, and soon after that he would go out to the pub.

Towards the end of junior school, relations between my parents were becoming strained. My brother and I noticed my mother became more independent, passing her driving test and becoming a county councillor; this meant even more time away from home, and tea was often a note Sellotaped to the microwave door saying '3 minutes on full power' and two other plated meals covered up at the side with the same note attached.

Throughout my junior school years, on odd occasions, I hid in the airing cupboard at home and spent the time in there wearing my mother's clothes and her shoes, which were a country mile too big for my tiny feet. I never got caught, and whilst wearing her clothes, which was like wearing a tent, I felt cosy, I felt myself, and I felt relaxed. In summary, whilst dressing in my mother's clothes, it felt natural, even normal, almost like those were the type of clothes I should be wearing instead of the boys' clothes I had to wear.

As the 1970s gave way to the 1980s, I started grammar school. All the other boys of my age had started to fill out their frames and become more masculine in appearance, some even looked like they had started to grow stubble on their faces and a few already had their deeper, manly voice. Not me: I was still skinny and scrawny and still looked quite feminine alongside the other boys. The girls were developing too and their breasts were growing, which left me thinking, *Where are mine?*

At grammar school the bullying got worse and became physical, too, ranging from a punch in the face to being kicked to the ground. My father's response was to tell me to stand up and hit them back; I tried just once and got beaten to a pulp.

I concentrated on school sports: it worked for me in junior school, lessening the bullying, and it worked at grammar school. I even managed to become good enough to play for the school team at football and cricket and, unbeknown to many, I learned to run, to run fast when running away from a potential beating.

But as the years progressed at grammar school, I soon found out that the main bullies were those who were in the lower forms, those who struggled and got poor grades, and the physical bullying got worse. On one occasion, a couple of thugs managed to dangle me out of a first-floor window. I don't ever think for one minute that they intended to drop me, and they didn't, but at the time I didn't know that and I was petrified.

After that incident, I decided to try and make people laugh by being the joker; everyone likes a comedian, don't they? In woodwork classes, which I hated as I wanted to do home economics, the first thing I did to raise a laugh was to saw halfway through the wooden handles of all the mallets in the tool cupboard. Shortly afterwards our tutor called us all round to do a demonstration; you've guessed it, a demonstration using a mallet and chisel. As he struck the first blow with the mallet, the head fell off!

He muttered something like, 'I don't know my own strength,' and grabbed another mallet. The next blow met with same result, at which point he then inspected each mallet.

'OK, which joker has done this?' Silence followed; I thought better of owning up, but it raised a good laugh. 'Nobody is leaving this room until the culprit owns up!' he shouted.

It was very nearly break time and a boy called Johnson said, 'It was me, sir.' WHAT! It was me, and this boy took the credit for my handiwork and instantly earned the respect of all his classmates. He got punished for it, and I still got bullied.

Again, in woodwork, a subject I never wanted to do, and indeed I never once did my homework for it either, we were all sat at our desks and the tutor handed back everyone's homework books. Except mine, that is; he got his big black marking book out and read out, 'Ashton, I have not got a single mark in here for you this term, if I don't see your homework book next week, you'll be paying a visit to the headmaster.' I later changed my surname from Ashton to Kelly when I filled in my deed poll to change my name to Lisa.

Everyone feared old wobble-head, as we used to call him, so I hatched a plan to avoid the headmaster. That plan would take a few weeks, but the first opportunity I got was during that same lesson. The tutor left the room for five minutes; we knew he was going outside to smoke, so while he was out, I grabbed his marking book and, using a red pen, entered marks next to my name for all the missing weeks.

The following week, without even looking in his book, he said, 'Ashton, where's your homework book?' Quick as a flash I responded with, 'At home, sir, sorry.'

Everyone knew what I'd done, and the tutor went on, 'You know what I told you last week—'

'But sir, it's the first time I've forgotten my homework,' I interrupted. With that, he checked his marking book, and sure enough he fell for it. I knew he would cotton on to what I had done at some point, so that lesson, while he was out smoking again, I took his big book and nailed it to the underneath of his desk. Again, everyone saw me do it, and it kept them off my back, at least for the time being.

My cunning plan worked for a week, and would probably have worked longer but for Johnson trying to keep the respect he'd gained from the mallet incident. He took a saw to the tutor's desk and sawed through each leg about halfway down. The desk remained upright until the tutor sat on it and it came tumbling down. Johnson got huge respect from his classmates, and because of the book now being visible and someone grassing me up, I copped the blame for the desk, and gained no respect, and so the bullying recommenced.

I meandered my way through grammar school in the same vein for the next couple of years, and the bullying steadily increased as my body still refused to fill out into a more masculine form and my voice broke. I say broke: it went down slightly but remained very much a soft, almost feminine, voice.

I also took every opportunity I got to wear underwear or skirts, skiving off physical education to go to the girls' changing room and put their skirts on while they were having their physical education lessons. Without exception, I always felt shame afterwards, a sense of guilt. Guilt at wearing the skirts, but guilt at the fact that I was violating another person in some way. I had no right to even enter those changing rooms and even less right to wear any of the clothing in them.

At the end of my penultimate year at school, there was the annual sports day and the cross-country run.

In every year before that I always jogged around, doing one lap and resting in the woods smoking and then rejoining the run as if I was on the final lap and trailing in among the last few finishers, but that year I decided to actually run all three laps and boy, did I run. From previous years of finishing nearly last I ran like the wind and finished in the top twenty, a feat that earned lots of complimentary comments, and when asked by one teacher how come I'd improved so much when I had previously shown so little ability, my reply was curt and to the point: 'When you get a choice between running away or being beaten up, you learn to run faster than the bully.'

My final year at school saw an end to me being bullied. For the first and only time in my life I snapped. One week in the final term, I got beaten up on the Monday by one boy, then the same boy hit me again on the Tuesday, and again on the Wednesday. He came for me on the Thursday, but this time it wasn't in a cloakroom where nobody could see, it was in the courtyard while everyone was playing or eating during the dinner break.

He came at me and went to hit me, but for once I knew what was coming and I ducked. He missed and I just swung my arm as hard as I could; my clenched fist landed on his nose and sent him crashing to the floor with blood pouring from his nose. All my pent-up anger at the countless beatings I'd taken came flooding out and while he was down I jumped on him and laid punch after punch on his face.

When a teacher dragged me off him it was plain to see that my bully had a broken nose. I had blackened both his eyes, which were swollen almost shut, and split his lip in several places.

I was suspended from school for the rest of the week and for the following week, the final week of our school term. It was the end of term and after the full term break we only returned to school on the days when our exams were scheduled to take place, our O levels as they were called back then. I was told that, for each of the exams I returned for, I would need to report to reception and be escorted to the exam, and then afterwards escorted off the school premises.

Exams were taken, and we began our summer holidays, or what used to be our summer holidays; now it was just summer and my father declared, 'Now you've left school, you're an adult, find a job or sign on the dole, but you now pay for your board and lodgings.'

It didn't take me long to get a summer job. I increased my hours at the fish and chip shop that I had been working at for the past two years, and found a YTS position at the brewery, which would start in September. YTS was the government's Youth Training Scheme.

I now had money for the first time and I was able to buy some clothes to keep in my room, and my dressing started in earnest.

Two

Early adulthood

At seventeen years of age I was still living at home, still in a small town, it was now the mid-eighties and back then the internet was still a pipe dream, and I was dressing more and more.

I felt different and I knew I shouldn't be a male. Maybe I was female? My puberty had been short-lived and started at fourteen and by seventeen I had stopped growing and puberty stopped too. I found it hard to understand why my chest hadn't grown like the girls' chests had done.

When my voice broke, it went down in tone and pitch by only a fraction and I stood at a 'massive' five feet four inches tall and pulled the scales all the way round to eight stone. I certainly looked anything but a man, but here I was just a few short months away from turning eighteen and becoming a man in the eyes of the world.

I didn't know the term for it back it then, and I also didn't know there were thousands like me up and down the country, but I was transgender, and I felt so alone in the world. It made me feel like I was a weirdo, like I was not normal, so I went through phases of trying my best to abstain from dressing. By now it wasn't just underwear, I had progressed onto skirts and blouses too. I hadn't yet dabbled with make-up or wigs, but then my hair was still long enough to brush into a feminine style.

In a bid to try and be normal, I found myself a girlfriend. She lived in the same street, and I can't claim it was love, it was more like fulfilling what was expected of a man, but I cared for her and loved her in a sisterly way. The relationship petered out, but we stayed friends.

We were still living in the days of extreme homophobia and the AIDS virus was getting the wrong type of publicity. In those days, people were claiming you could catch it from sitting on the toilet seat and other such crass rumours. Racism was still rife and prejudice towards any person considered 'not normal' ran wild.

In those days, the tormentors I'd grown up with had moved on to calling disabled people 'cabbages', black people 'niggers', and the poorer people of the community were called 'gypos', a derogatory term for a gypsy.

By and large the bullying I used to receive had died down to just verbal abuse in the pubs. Had they known about my inclination for dressing as a woman, I dare say I would have been beaten to within an inch of my life and run out of town.

I lost my virginity to my first girlfriend, and for about a year I abstained from dressing, but the thought never left me and the urge never receded, it only grew. The more I abstained, the more the urge to dress controlled me and the more my mood would turn downwards towards depression. I reached the point at nineteen when I got depressed but didn't know why. I was constantly feeling down, but carried on with work and my social life; I just thought that sometimes you felt down and depressed as an adult.

Then I put my clothes on for the first time in over a year, and the depression lifted almost instantly. I felt happy wearing women's clothes. I never felt anything remotely sexual, it was never sexually exciting for me to dress, but still I had no idea that I was not alone in being a man that wore ladies' clothes.

Naturally enough, I grew moody. I wanted to dress every day, but I couldn't. I didn't have the privacy, and I had a girlfriend too. My moodiness slowly eroded that relationship away, and I was back to being single.

Around that time, I finally found out that I was not the only person who dressed. In the local paper, I saw a headline: 'Tadcaster Man has Sex Change'. He, or rather she, had been outed and been hounded out of town. It made me even more scared to tell anyone how I really felt, or let anyone catch me whilst dressed.

I started venturing to some local woods so that I could dress outdoors. I wanted to be able to walk outdoors while dressed, and the woods were perfect. After several visits without seeing another soul, I grew ever more confident and walked freely through the woods whilst dressed, and then one day someone else was there, a man possibly in his thirties. He was just standing around, but he'd seen me.

Panic set in. He was between me and my scooter, between me and my male clothes. He started to make his way towards me, and I had nowhere to go. He stopped at the side of a tree about twenty yards from me and I could see him touching his groin area. I couldn't move, I had nowhere to go and was too scared to walk past him. I didn't know him, but he might easily have known me.

After a couple of minutes, he came right up to me and whilst stroking his penis through his tracksuit bottoms he asked, 'What are you into?'

'What do you mean?' I nervously replied.

'You know,' he paused. 'Wanking, blow jobs, sex.'

Being naïve and thinking he meant what I liked doing with women I answered, 'Sex and blow jobs.'

There was no disguising the fact that I was a guy dressed as a woman. He reached forward and put his hand behind my head, pulling me forward and downwards slightly. 'Start sucking on this then,' he commanded in a strong voice while getting his penis out with his free hand.

I tried to pull away, but he was much bigger and stronger than me, and he forced me to my knees, and forced my head down onto his penis. What followed, I tried to blank out of my mind as I was first forced to give him a blow job, and then he buggered me; he raped me. I cried with the pain and I cried all the way through it, and when he finished and went away, I just lay there very distressed and cried like a baby for about an hour.

I got into my male clothing, left my female clothing behind and went home, weeping all the way, as soon as I got home, I got in the bath and scrubbed myself clean. I still felt dirty though and I struggled to get my head round what had happened. I still felt the pain even though the physical pain had gone. I went to my bedroom and curled up in a ball on my bed and sobbed.

I never told a soul, I never dressed again for over two years, and each day for about two months after being raped, I just went to work, came home from work and went to my room, where I just stayed and cried.

In hindsight I was stupid. I mean, I didn't think that men suffered the torment of rape, they do, and almost always it goes unreported, but I had put myself in position of being vulnerable, I had been too naïve to realise that I was in danger and it could have turned out far worse. I could so easily have ended up in hospital or even dead. I hadn't known at the time, but at nineteen years old, I was under the legal age of consent for sex between men.

Nobody, male or female, should suffer the brutality of rape. If I had known that I was at risk, I would have had something with me to try to get myself out that situation, something like pepper spray, or a panic alarm. On top of all that, I was also blind to the dangers of sexually transmitted disease. Thankfully, when I was checked out at a much later date, I was all clear, but after the trauma of being raped, even if I was far too scared to report it, I should have had my health checked out at the very least.

Gradually I started to venture out again, to the pub, and got drunk almost every night I went out. I got verbally abused in the pubs, and each time I just stood up, walked out and went to the next pub.

In a drunken haze one night I walked a girl home, we sneaked into her room, kissed, had sex, and I went home, and the following morning I cried. I don't know why I cried; maybe it was because it my first sexual contact of any kind since I had been raped, maybe it was just through sheer delight, but whatever the reason, I sat and I cried.

It took me two years to even think about buying some more clothes, but that urge never leaves you, it never relents, it eats away at you, and finally I bought some clothes again.

I met another girl in the pub some weeks later. We got on quite well and kind of bounced off each other a little bit, I wouldn't say I fell in love with her, more of a comfort type of friendship. We met a few times and started dating, me hiding my cross-dressing ways from her, and we went steady for a couple of years, but my urge to have sexual relations with her dried up, it was down to me needing to find more time to dress.

After several months being sexless, she told me she was six months pregnant. The baby could not possibly have been mine, and we split up. A few months after her daughter was born she asked to see me. Reluctantly, I agreed. I fell in love with the baby and we got back together. We got together for all the wrong reasons; she really did love me, but I never loved her, I loved her daughter and looked on her as if she was my own. I felt like a mother and for the first time, I realised I wanted to be a mother, not a father.

We bought a house with help from our parents, and soon after, got married. I was now twenty-four going on twenty-five and my paltry eight stone in weight had gone up to nine stone seven pounds, and for the next fifteen years my weight would fluctuate between this and ten stone.

Soon after that my brother also moved out, and shortly afterwards, my parents split up, and I slid into depression once again. I was working twelve hours a day, and coming home to do the housework. My wife was not working and lived her life as though she was in a pig sty: a pig sty that I was coming home to each day and having to clean up. I couldn't dress, and I couldn't cope.

I tried my hardest to look after the daughter that I thought of as my own and loved, but I could not do it alone whilst working all the hours I was to pay the bills whilst her mother sat in her rubbish dump. I wanted her out of the house, but she wouldn't go.

I started to see someone from work and spent most of my nights at the pub with her, after doing the housework, just so I wasn't in the same place as my wife, who had turned into a slob. Then, through the girls at work, I got the chance to dress and go out in public. They had been daring the other two lads to go on a night out dressed up. There were three males at my workplace, and about ten women, and the other two men chickened out, but bold as brass, I said I'd do it.

On the night in question, I went around to one of the girls' houses and a couple of them helped to dress me; they did my make-up and put a lovely wig on me. By now my hair was short, almost a skinhead, but the wig looked amazing on me, and very lifelike too. I looked every inch a female by the time they'd finished, and we all walked to the meeting point, the pub.

There, we got a minibus to a restaurant and we sat down for a meal. I sat opposite the girl I was seeing, Donna. I had earlier been introduced as the cousin of one of the other girls, and they had told Donna that I couldn't make it. They all knew we were seeing each other, so it was a test for her to see if she'd recognise me. While we chatted, I was putting on a softer voice and for about an hour she thought nothing was wrong. Then I said, 'Don't you recognise me?' She took a close look, a lingering look, then responded with, 'No, should I?' In my normal voice I said, 'It's me, Dave!'

Well, you could have knocked out an elephant with the look she had on her face, it was one of sheer disbelief and shock, but also of anger. Her eyes just kind of froze and her face lost its colour, everyone at our table burst out laughing, including myself.

She was not amused at all, and didn't speak to me for a couple of hours, by which time we had returned by minibus back to our small town and gone into the first pub en route to the town centre. It happened to be my local pub, and I knew many people in there, but I went unrecognised by them.

Finally, whilst there, Donna spoke to me again, 'Don't ever do that to me again, you bastard!'

After we chatted a while it turned out that she was embarrassed at her own failure to recognise the person she had been cheating on her husband with, and with everyone laughing, including me, it had made her feel insecure, self-conscious and a little bit angry too. She had thought she was the butt of the joke, and she hadn't liked it.

In the next pub that we moved onto, some guy I'd never seen before came over to where I was stood chatting with Donna, and started to join our chat, buying us both a drink, and trying to edge Donna out of the conversation and chatting to me.

Thoughts began to run through my mind. I wasn't giving any thought to the fact that he could turn nasty, even violent, should he find out that I was not actually female. No, I was thinking, *Wow, this guy thinks I'm a woman and is actually chatting me up.*

It made me feel good and was a massive boost to my confidence, but I was also thinking how I could get Donna back into the conversation. Donna by now was glaring at me with eyes that could kill. Finally, I ended the conversation with the stranger by saying, 'Look honey, if you're after getting into my knickers, you're out of luck, I'm a lesbian,' and I quickly made my way to a table, taking Donna with me.

The rest of our group had already moved onto the next pub, so we finished our drinks and set off to rejoin our group. Along the way, Donna was slightly cold towards me. She later confided in one of the other girls, that me getting chatted up at her expense had made her feel like a gooseberry, and she wasn't at all happy that she was overlooked in favour of a guy in a dress.

On joining the rest of our group, unbeknown to me, they had cajoled some guy into chatting me up for a laugh. This guy was fully aware of what I was; he was doing it thinking he might get lucky with one of the other girls. I knew no different, and again it felt great to be taken for a female, it boosted my confidence in dressing no end, but Donna was fuming. When the guy went to the bar for the next round of drinks, she stormed over to me and demanded I go home and get changed back into a male; otherwise it was off between us.

It's harsh saying it now, but back then Donna was my release valve from my own failing marriage, and a way to keep myself out the depression that followed my desire to dress, like a lamb following its mother. So rather than risk losing my release valve,

I went to the girl's house where I had got changed, and changed back into the dull drab male that I was, a somewhat shy, nervous skinny lad who looked like he'd been at the back of the queue when puberty was handed out to the other boys.

Returning once again to join our group, I was no longer anyone's focus of attention, and I was no longer a confident, vibrant person. I stood on the edge of the group. Donna was decidedly frosty towards me, and I pretty much remained quiet for what was left of the evening.

Donna's own marriage had been failing long before I got involved with her, and when she finally left her husband and got a council flat, I moved in with her. Everything was great for a few months, she even took me to meet her family, who lived near the coast, but not everything was going well, bubbling under the surface I had my own demons. I still had a burning desire to dress, and an overwhelming need to express my true self.

At this point in time, the internet was just being born, but still far away from my reach. I also found out that the nights that Donna went out, supposedly with some of the girls from work, and I stayed home to dress in private, in safety, without her knowledge, she was seeing other guys. She had a secret, I had a secret, something was going to give at some point, and boy did it give!

She didn't do a fantastic job at hiding her secret, but I turned a blind eye. I had opportunities to dress whilst she out with her latest fella. I kept my secret extremely well hidden, until one night when she came home early and caught me wearing her clothes. She took it extremely badly, there was no shouting, just silence,

'Look, I don't mind you seeing other men,' I cried, it was a last-ditch effort to try and get some words from her. I was letting her know that both our little secrets were now known to each other, in the hope that we could sit and talk to each other, but she picked up a bottle and bolted into the bedroom, locking herself in. I pleaded with her to let me in so we could talk, I pleaded for her to come out so we could talk, but it kept landing on deaf ears.

I slumped down at the side of the door and began to sob, and then I heard her trying to open a jar of pills. *Oh, my God, no.* I started to plead with her again, only this time I was pleading for her not to take any pills. I heard another jar being opened, my pleading became frantic, desperate, I kept up relentlessly trying to coax her out, trying to stop her from taking pills, I never stopped for nearly an hour, when I did pause for breath, I heard nothing, the bedroom was silent.

I knew then that I had to act, and act quickly. I phoned for the ambulance and then broke the lock on the door. Lord only knows where I found the strength to break the lock, but somehow, I did.

She was lying on the bed, semi-conscious. I struggled to get her to her feet, but somehow I managed it. I was running on pure adrenalin and I began to walk her around the flat. I knew from first aid training that I needed to keep her moving and keep her awake, and if possible to try and induce her to vomit. The ambulance guys soon arrived and took over. I went with them in the ambulance and stayed all night at her side. I called her family to let them know what had happened, missing out the details of events leading up to it of course.

She was soon out of any danger after having her stomach pumped, and once I was sure she was OK, I made my way home, for sleep and food, ready to return in the afternoon or early evening. I spent the evening chatting with her, both of us avoiding the subject of the previous night, and when visiting time ended, I went home to bed.

Around lunchtime the following day, I got a call from one of Donna's brothers. 'Donna's staying with us for a few days, we are just setting off to the flat, you've got just over an hour to get your stuff and get out, and if we ever see your tranny arse again, we will kill you!' With that matter-of-fact statement, the phone went dead.

Blind panic followed. I knew what her brothers were like, and I knew they never made idle threats. Whether they would kill me, I doubted, but I was certain that they would break both my legs and arms at the very least; I knew at least two of them had served time at Her Majesty's pleasure for GBH.

With little option, I gathered what I could and got out damn sharpish. I'd made a quick call to my mother who by now was divorced from my father and had her own two-bedroomed flat.

I settled there in the spare room and lived like a recluse for a few months, eating nothing but junk food, and going through the motions at work. I was in a deep depression yet again; a life trauma had triggered it, but the underlying problem was me: I still felt very much different to normal people, but by now I was starting to think along the lines of, '*Maybe I am just in the wrong body*' and '*Maybe I was supposed to have been born female*'.

With these thoughts, and staying at my mother's flat, I had zero chance to dress, which did nothing to help my depression. But Mother, being a county councillor, had a desktop computer, which had access to the World Wide Web.

Three

The age of discovery

At long last I could research my problem. I spent many hours looking up men who dressed as women, and I encountered the official terminology for people like me. I found out that those like me fell into more than category; at that point, I didn't know what category to place myself into. A cross-dresser and a transvestite fell pretty much into the same category, with a few minor details between the two, but basically, they both were men who dressed in women's clothing, some for sexual thrills, some just pretend to be female, but both were occasional dressers.

A transsexual was different: although they too dressed as female, they did it to try to be as close to female as they could, they did it more than occasionally, and for many they did it almost full-time.

At that stage of life, just shy of thirty years old, I classed myself as a cross-dresser. At that stage, it was still an occasional thing for me to do, and I still didn't bother with make-up or wigs. I wasn't trying to look the part, I just did it because I felt comfortable in those clothes, I felt normal, like it was a natural thing for me to do.

It was around this time of my life that I first started to wonder what it would be like to be a woman. I knew by then that people could have a sex change operation, but until then I just naïvely assumed that one day you go into hospital, have an operation, and come out as woman... albeit a woman only on the outside. I had no idea how they gave you breasts and a vagina, but I knew they could not give you a womb and that they had to 'chop off' your penis.

I just had to find out, so I trawled the internet. Information on sex changes was sketchy to say the least, but at last I found out that it was not as simple as going into hospital, having the 'op' and coming out female, and that it was known as gender reassignment surgery.

There was a method that had to be followed, it was like an unwritten law, but it had to be done a certain way, following a certain route as laid down by the NHS. Could I take that route? I was still in that small town where just about everyone knew everyone else, my schooldays bullies still lived there and were still just as obnoxious as they had been at school. I had seen the headline in the local paper a few years before, and I just knew I would be destined for the same fate if I were to change sex.

By now it was the late '90s and the world was waking up to racism and hate crimes, but in my small town there were still a great number of bigots. If I were to follow the NHS route to becoming a woman, I certainly could not do it in that town. The route laid down was this: first you go to your GP and tell him you have mixed-up feelings about your gender. At this stage, nobody else knows about you, unless you've told them yourself. Your GP refers you to a local therapist for a quick assessment, and based on what you tell you them over a few sessions, or even just a single session, that therapist will then refer you to the local area's gender hospital for further assessments, or the therapist will refuse to refer you any further, and you remain in limbo.

It is at the gender hospital assessment stage that you have an assessment, and are told you'll get another assessment in a few months, by which time they expect you to have changed your name by deed poll and be living full-time as a woman; they called it the real-life experience.

Of course, it would be at that stage that my secret would be out. If I did this, how on earth could I live a real-life experience? It would be an open invitation to the bigots and bullies to focus on me once again.

I stopped researching along those lines at that point, so I missed other details that I would need to know eventually, but for now, I was stuck not yet fully knowing who or what I was, and not knowing what to do with my life. The one thing that remained constant throughout that time was my desire to dress, coupled with my depressions when I could not dress.

My research did show me that I was not alone at all, that there were lots of people like me, and that people like me went to varying locations away from home in order to meet. It didn't tell me what happened at these meeting places, but often they took place in woodland, and memories of my last visit to some woods came flooding back. I was never going back to any woods to dress ever again. The memories were too painful, and I was also too scared of the same thing or something similar happening again. So I was back at square one, no place to dress, and no chance to follow the path that, back then, I did not actually know that I would one day need to follow.

I did find one thing on the internet though, quite by accident: I found chat rooms where you could 'chat' to anyone who happened to be online. I spent many hours chatting to other people about anything and everything, but I never got involved on the subject of sex and sexuality, that is until one day chatting to someone who, like me, appeared to spend an awful lot of time online.

We had been chatting for weeks when he made an astounding revelation right out of the blue: he just came straight out with it and said that he liked to wear women's clothes. Well, I was in my element now, and we chatted for hours, days, weeks. Eventually he suggested we meet and have fun dressing together in the safety of his house. A date was set when he would have the house to himself and I went around there.

After a coffee and chat we both stripped off and proceeded to put on our female attire. I didn't feel the need to dress in private; after all, we were only having fun dressing up. He put a porn film on, but I wasn't really interested in that, I carried on trying on the variety of clothes that I had taken with me, but eventually I did sit down, and we chatted again. It was during this chat that he came out and asked me outright, 'Can I give you a kiss?'

I had never kissed another guy before. My only experience of anything remotely sexual with another guy was that horrendous experience when I was raped in the woods. I didn't reply; instead I just burst into tears. I tearfully tried to explain to him that I had endured a terrible ordeal with another man, and that I was scared he would do the same. He quickly apologised and asked me if I wanted to change back into my male clothes. I nodded a yes and he said, 'Go into the bathroom and change, and I'll make us another cuppa.'

Once I had changed, we sat and chatted again. I explained that I had never willingly done anything with another guy, not even kissed, and that my dressing was something that I didn't do for sexual kicks. He was very nice about it all and constantly kept apologising, also telling me that he too had not so much as kissed another guy before, but that he was strangely attracted to me and he didn't know why.

Suddenly I felt kind of safe again, and I'll admit to being flattered that some guy could find me attractive; I don't know why, but I leant in and kissed his cheek. The next thing I knew, we were kissing each other.

Soon we were having sex: gay sex. I was in a daze. It was all happening so fast and as much as I wanted to stop, something kept urging me to carry on, damn it, I should not have been enjoying it, I had no reason to like having any form of sex with another guy, but I was.

Afterwards once I had returned home, I began to feel ashamed of myself. I felt embarrassed, I felt high, I felt down, I felt elated; God, I had so many emotions racing around my head, but one thing that I knew for certain, I liked sex with women, and now I liked sex with men.

From there I started to look up information about gender dysphoria again. I needed more answers and I had stopped my research too early some months previously.

I found out that, after a second consultation, I would possibly be prescribed a low dosage of female hormones. To my horror, I also found out that the timeline from first seeing my local GP to that second consultation could be as much as eighteen months, and that only about a year after being prescribed hormones would I even be considered for breast augmentation surgery, and then up to a further two years before full gender reassignment surgery, the final operation where they remove your penis and make a vagina out of the penile skin and scrotum.

That alone almost put me off, but what really stopped me from starting the process was a reality check in the pub, my first venture to any social venue for well over a year. The same old obnoxious bullies were there, almost as if they were all part of the furniture, and I got a stark reminder of my school days when the verbal abuse started. I went to the landlord and complained, but the response I got was, 'They spend a lot more money in here than you; if you don't like it go somewhere else.' I did go somewhere else: I went home.

As 1999 became 2000 and heralded the new millennium, I finally got a flat; well, I moved in with a woman, but it got me away from living with my mother and I was finally able to resume my dressing in the privacy of home, when I knew it was safe. My doom and gloom lifted as I also started to experiment with make-up. My comical attempts at applying eyeshadow had to be seen to be believed, and my expertise in applying lipstick was almost as funny, but I was learning, and nobody else was ever going to see what a mess I was making. It took time and patience applying make-up and getting it halfway decent, well, what I thought was halfway decent. I only had memories of the internet now, I didn't have my own computer and my phone internet was pretty much useless.

Looking back, had I chosen to venture out whilst dressed complete with make-up, I would have been instantly uncovered as a 'tranny'.

Four

The noughties

The first thing of note about the noughties was getting my divorce finalised, apart from selling the matrimonial home: that, I couldn't do until my ex-wife's daughter reached adulthood.

My dressing continued during my leisure time, and I continued to practice with make-up, but looking back, the clothes I chose and the make-up I applied just looked trashy and bloody awful to be brutally honest, but at the time I thought I looked OK.

I began to realise that, in order to resolve my life, I would have to leave that small town I had called home for almost all my life, but the chance to get away never reared its head, and so my depression once again returned.

I continued to explore my own sexuality, and armed with a newer mobile phone, I was now able to get better internet access. I found a kinky website, one that opened my eyes to the world of BDSM. Foolishly, I first thought that BDSM was just kinky sex; it was far from it, but in that little world I made friends, something I had struggled to do.

A brief history of my small band of friends goes like this: one year, not long before my birthday, my best friend from school died aged just thirty-four; he had got drunk and gone to sleep at his flat and choked on his own vomit. He been dead a few days before anyone found him. Another of my school friends had a fatal car accident just before my birthday; he died aged twenty-five. In the early 1990s, just before my birthday, my grandfather on my mother's side passed away. In the late nineties, his widow, my gran, passed away, and it wasn't that long after my birthday. Early in the noughties, in the summertime, my other grandfather passed away. My only remaining grandparent hung on and on; we all knew she was waiting for what would have been her late husband's birthday, and on that day, she too passed away, two days before my own birthday.

Back to my new friends, I soon discovered they were all far more honest and trustworthy than my previous friends, barring just a couple. At events that they held, I could dress in public, albeit a closed public, but I could dress and have lots of other people see me and not judge me; they all accept you for who you are, not what you are; if you show them politeness and honesty, you are treated with politeness and honesty, and mutual respect grows.

I really was in my element, I had a bunch of new friends who didn't care that I looked like a trashy tranny, they treated me the same as they treated anyone else, with dignity, respect and kindness. As time passed and more new friends were made, some people even offered tips and help on make-up and such.

Of course, the depression was never far away. Despite my new friends and new-found happiness, I was still feeling lost within myself. As I talked to people whom I now regarded as my friends, I began to realise that, if you want something out of life, you must make it happen, it won't just come to you. Each time I found myself depressed, I got through it by getting my head down and working, but also by whistling tunes, singing songs and trying to make others laugh. Each time, slowly but surely, I crawled out of my depression.

My bouts of depression largely went unnoticed by other people; they always thought that I was happy and cheerful, due to me singing and joking to lift my gloom.

By the late noughties, I was working on the outskirts of the city of York, away from the small town that had consumed my life. It meant I now finally had a chance to get away from town life, but I needed money to do it. There always seemed to be a 'but' in everything I wanted or tried to do. I started saving what I could each month, but it seemed that every time my savings got past a few hundred pounds, something went wrong! An unexpected bill, an appliance to buy, motorbike repairs, or a couple of weeks on the sick; something always reared up and ate away what I had saved. The 'but' that got in the way always torpedoed my self-esteem and knocked my confidence, and always, without fail, sank me right back into the depths of depression.

Finally, though, as the decade ended, my fortunes slowly picked up. I managed to get through 2010 without hitting any obstacles, I finally had a depression-free year, and my savings were slowly inching towards being able to move out my jail; that small town had very much become a jail to me. It was like I had finally served my time and was now just awaiting the parole board to approve my release.

Five

A new start

2011 began on a massive downward spiral: in mid January, my best friend took his own life. I struggled to come to terms with what he had done; nobody had the slightest idea that he was depressed, much like my own depression that I kept covered up.

I found myself questioning the reasoning behind his suicide, Despite my own depression, I could not get my head around why he had taken his own life. We had made plans the day before to go fishing. He'd never caught anything bigger than a few ounces, and I knew where we could go to rectify that; he was genuinely looking forward to going. We had the whole day planned: at lunchtime, after a morning of fishing, we would go to his local pub for Sunday lunch, then have an afternoon of drinking and watching the live band that was due to play at the pub.

I was truly lost; he was the last of my friends away from the world of BDSM. My own depression returned and I spent nearly a month getting drunk every night. My rescue came in the form of an offer of a house in the city, an offer completely out of the blue, and it was an offer to house-share with a couple of friends from the world of BDSM. We would be renting privately, but at long last I had a release, a way out of the prison that had kept me captive far longer than a prisoner serving a sentence for murder.

At the end of April 2011, I moved to York, I had a new lease of life, and after the first couple of months flying high, my thoughts returned to my inner self, that overwhelming feeling that had been with me throughout my life, the feeling of not actually being male, but a freak of nature that had put a woman into the body of a man, my body, me.

I finally got my house sold after settling for far less than I should have got for it, but I now had money too, not millions, just a couple of thousand, which took no time at all to blow. I splashed out on a new computer, and clothes, male and female; I got a new TV, had lots of takeaways instead of cooking, I bought all manner of things that I didn't really need. I suppose too that I binged a little bit too much on fast food and takeaways: my weight ballooned to just under twelve stone.

I soon realised that you should never go on a wild spending spree, because once you start, it's very hard to stop and you buy lots of stuff that you do not need. That year simply flew past, it almost overtook me and left me behind, it went that fast. Work was going better than it had ever gone before, and when I finally caught up with 2011, it was ending, and 2012 was coming at me head on.

Bloody hell, 2012 already, I was now 43 and I had done nothing with my life, I had not resolved my lifelong issue, nor even started to take control of it. If there was one thing that the death of my best friend had taught me, it was not to dwell on the past, but live for today, live life and try your damnedest to enjoy it. I bought myself some prosthetic breasts that were worn like a bra; they felt as real as you could with fakes, and these were the same type that women who had mastectomies wore. They had a natural bounce to them, they felt almost real to the touch, and if they weren't cold you could easily mistake them for real when touched.

As with everything about my life, there was always something waiting in the wings to kick me, and sure enough, just when my life was looking up and I was genuinely looking forward to life, it happened. My mother's partner of ten years died suddenly. It hit my mother very hard; it also knocked me for six. Typically, I sank once more into the depths of depression, yet through it, I constantly tried to help my mother, as did the rest of my family.

At the same time, the couple out of the house-share separated, and we were suddenly looking at having to move. I was becoming more and more stressed by what was happening with my life; work took a steep dive downwards as the night shift was disbanded and I found myself sharing my own team with the supervisor from nights. She was an absolute bitch to work alongside, away from work a very nice person, but at work she would happily stab you in the back and laugh as she twisted the knife.

Slowly but surely my work life got me down. To heap yet more misery onto me, we were rapidly approaching the most stressful time at work: the stocktake. The way things were panning out, the house move was to be on the morning of the day of our work stocktake. Jeez, I was already depressed and feeling down and stressed, and this just added that bit extra on top.

We got the move from one side of the city to the other side of the city done and dusted quite smoothly, but I had no time to unpack nor make my bed, because it was stocktake. I had no chance of taking any time off like people normally do when moving to a new house. I dashed off to work, and the stocktake, my stress levels rising like the flood waters of rain-filled rivers.

During the stocktake, I took a phone call; it was a very bad line, but I could make out it was my aunty, and she was telling me that my mother was in hospital. The line went dead; I had no idea if it was serious, and I couldn't get through when I tried to call back. It was only about fifteen minutes until tea break, so I left it, to try again at break. In those fifteen minutes my mind was racing and the stress was now really getting to me.

I tried in vain to get some answers; my aunty was not answering her phone, and they wouldn't tell me anything over the phone when I tried the hospital. I joined the rest of my colleagues for break and they were all laughing and joking, and some of the subject matter of their jokes was old folk being coffin-dodgers and oxygen-thieves. Well, I snapped; I verbally laid into one of them, giving him a torrent of home truths and some 'ad-libs' as quickly as it happened. I forget what the ad libs were that I threw into the abuse, but as soon as I left the canteen and went back to work I started to regret saying them, not the home truths, but the bits I threw in as extras. I knew what I'd said could land me in trouble, but right there and then I just needed some severe stress relief, and some news of my mother.

From work, I could only go home; it was gone midnight and I knew a trip to the hospital would be met with nothing. I slept very badly, despite being extremely tired, almost exhausted, and as soon as humanely possible, well, as soon it could be deemed a reasonable hour of the day, I started to phone people for answers.

My aunty wasn't answering, but then she was never an early riser, so I didn't read too much into it. The hospital would not tell me anything at all, saying I could very well be this person's son, but I could just as easily be a stranger fishing for anything newsworthy, and in my stressed-out state, I lost my cool with them. I mean, who wouldn't? I had had the day from hell the day before, the stress I was feeling was unbearable, I was extremely tired, I had everything still in boxes waiting to be unpacked save for a duvet and my work clothes and I had to work alongside someone who was systematically alienating my team from me, and all I wanted was the answer to a simple question: why was my mother in hospital and how serious was it?.

I was of course wasting my time over the phone with the hospital, so I decided I needed to get showered and get myself to the hospital, regardless of visiting times. Just before I was ready to leave the house, my phone rang. It was my brother. I never really got on with James: when he did something wrong as a child, it was me who always copped the blame, being the eldest. I grew to resent him for that, and things were not helped when he soon displayed all the signs of being a bully himself. We had many arguments in our early adulthood and grew further apart, to the point where, for the previous few years, our only interactions had been at family occasions like christenings, weddings and funerals as well as the social gatherings to celebrate family milestones like a cousin's eighteenth or a notable wedding anniversary. The one family celebration that I did miss out on was my brother's wedding. I was told about it, but I never received an invite.

The call from my brother James went something like this:

James: 'I thought you ought to know that Mum is in hospital and she won't be coming out.'
Me: 'What!? What's wrong with her? How long has she got?'
James: 'She's been in a week or so and it's her constant heavy drinking that has done it; her liver has suffered irreparable damage and has muddled her brain, it's just a matter of time.'
Me: 'What do you mean she's been in a week? Why the

fuck did no one tell me? And what do you call just a matter of time?'

James: 'The consultant says it could be days or even weeks, but you have to prepare yourself for the worst and go and say your goodbyes, she has no idea she is dying, so don't tell her, we have signed the 'Do not resuscitate' forms, so when she stops breathing, that will be it.'

I sat and cried. I cried because I was losing my mother, because I was fuming at the way my family had kept me in the dark about my mother, because I was so angry that if I didn't cry, I would explode in some other way. It took some time to compose myself so that I could go to the hospital and visit my mother, but during the trip to the hospital my only thoughts were: *What could I say to my mum? Should I tell her she was dying, or should I hold back and find some way to say goodbye without her reading too much into it?*

When I arrived at the hospital it dawned on me that I didn't even know where in the hospital she was. After a short wait at reception I was told which ward, so I headed there with a heavy heart and a lump in my throat. At the ward desk, I asked which room my mother was in, and was told that the consultant was just in with her if I would like to wait a few minutes; I took that opportunity to ask if I could speak to the consultant before I saw my mother. When the consultant came over to me, I had a barrage of questions I wanted to ask, and I fired them all at him one after another without pausing for the answers. I couldn't help it, my mind felt like it had a load of demented gerbils running around inside and the thoughts racing around were driving me to edge of my remaining sanity, if I had much sanity to start with!

The answers I got were somewhat different to how my brother had told it; he always did exaggerate and then added some more on top, so I really should not have been surprised. It turned out that my mother was in danger, but if she got through the week, then the outlook would improve. She did indeed have severe liver damage and she had also done irreversible damage to her brain, which meant that she would be permanently disorientated and not be fully aware of things. She would basically have no idea of what time zone she was in; she would think it was a particular day, week or year and in effect be living in the past.

As I entered the room where my mother was, my stomach was tied up in knots, and I used all my concentration on holding myself together. I couldn't allow myself to break down now, that had to wait until I was back home; right now I needed to stay calm and strong. My mother was sedated and drifting in and out of sleep, so conversation was out, it would just be a one-way conversation, me talking, and mother hopefully hearing what I said.

I told her I was sorry I hadn't been any sooner to see her, and then I chatted about work and moving to a new house. I left out the stress I was under, I talked about the weather and how lousy it was, how the garden was like a field at Glastonbury, and just general chit-chat. I ended by telling her that, no matter what, I loved her and always would.

I went home and cried my heart out. All my pent-up emotions came flooding out, I was surrounded by cardboard boxes in a strange house and as I cried, I thought to myself, *So much for a new start.*

Six

Things just had to change

Just a few hours after getting home from the hospital, I was back at work. My team was comprised of a mixed bunch of men and women, young and old; some of those men, the younger ones, had voiced various opinions about foreigners, lesbians, gays, cross-dressers, politics, sport and numerous other topics over the past few years, and I got the distinct impression that if they knew about the secret side of my life, they would make my work life hell.

 I knew that for things to change I would have to face them with my secret life, or find some other way to live my life without fear of my dirty great secret becoming public knowledge, but at that point I wasn't sure how I could do it. I had escaped the small town to possibly explore and carry out some options; now I found the work side of my life interfering, but I had to put all that on the back burner for now. I had more serious things going on in my life that I had to deal with first. I couldn't make any firm plans to do anything whilst I didn't know what was happening with my mother.

Anyhow, it was the day after stocktake, and an hour or so into my shift I was called into the manager's office. In the room was the assistant manager, whom I didn't get on with at all, and the admin person, the mother of one of the lads on my evening team. I was told by the assistant manager that it was informal and not recorded, and that I was being given a chance to apologise for what I had said the day before. I said I would like to know what words I was alleged to have used and to whom I needed to apologise; I had forgotten most of what I said but I was 90% certain that I had not mentioned anyone outside of my evening team, and wondered if I had upset someone with my language rather than the person I had hurled the abuse at.

The assistant manager said, 'You said that Carol had her tongue so far up my arse that her tongue and throat should be brown, so I want an apology, and so too does Carol.' Carol was the admin person.

I knew that I hadn't said that, at least I was pretty certain I hadn't said it, I had aimed a few things at one person on my team and everything I had hurled at him, home truth and add-ons, I just knew were all aimed at him and nobody else, so I stood firm and flatly denied saying those things, and that I certainly wouldn't apologise for something I had not done.

The assistant manager then said, 'I don't believe you, just apologise and it won't go any further.' He went on to add, 'If you don't apologise, I'll close this meeting, and Carol will write out her formal grievance against you, and that would mean disciplinary action being taken, and you could potentially lose your job.'

I stood firm.

'I will not apologise for something I have not done. Carol, you know me better than him, you know when I am wrong I hold my hands up and admit it, why would I stand here and lie?'

With that, the assistant manager sent me out of the office and back to work. I was now worried. A grievance would mean an investigation and witness statements, and I had enough people on my team who had already been alienated against me thanks to the former night supervisor, and I knew she would twist the knife too. After all, she was without her own team and this would pave the way for her to take over my team, and my job. I knew an investigation would mean I would be suspended; because all the investigation and statements would surround my team, I would be deemed as being able to influence the statements.

Somehow, I got through my shift without breaking down, but I was now under such huge stress and with depression sinking in too, I just couldn't cope. Next morning, I went straight to the doctor's and was signed off for two weeks with work-related stress and depression. For now, at least, I couldn't be suspended, nor could I be contacted in relation to the grievance. Should work do so, they would be in breach of the company policy and procedure.

It meant I could visit my mother daily, but also, I could now finally do my unpacking and turn this strange house into my new home. The remainder of that week was spent feeling rather sorry for myself, and worrying about my job. Right from the start I had made my bosses fully aware of my house move, and then of my mother's condition. I was flatly turned down time off on stocktake day, and at no point did anyone have the courtesy to even ask about my mother.

Later that day I was at the hospital again, visiting my mother, who had got through that first crucial week and was now having further tests. Whilst chatting to my mother, she could only tell me that she thought she had been shopping that morning, and had forgotten to put her Grand National bets on; the Grand National had been run the month before.

The consultant came and he spoke to both of us. He wanted me present because he knew my mother would not understand or even remember what he was saying.

'The CT scan has revealed no further damage, there's no improvement either, and the damage done is permanent. However, physically you are far better than when you first arrived and if you continue to show the same improvement, we can consider allowing you to go home in a week or so; you will need some home help once you're back at home, and we will arrange this for you.'

He went on, 'I must stress to you though, and I can't put enough emphasis on this, your liver is only partially functional and you will need dialysis every month. Should you return to drinking alcohol, your liver will fail and the damage to your brain will worsen. Think of George Best on his second liver, and where he is now; returning to drinking will kill you.'

As predicted, my mother did not comprehend any of what was said. I had a mix of emotions though; I was elated that soon my mother could go home, but I also knew that my mother wouldn't be able to stay off the booze. I just didn't know how long she would remain sober.

The stress under which I had been buried lifted, but I was still down in the dumps. I still had to change some aspect of my life, but what? I certainly wasn't looking forward to going back to work once my sick note ran out; over the past few months at work, I had gone from loving my job to hating it, and all because of the bitch woman, the night supervisor. She was a skiver, she talked a good talk, but never got stuck into the actual physical work, she constantly went missing from the area of work, and she was getting away with it. The assistant manager thought she was a perfect example of a supervisor, even suggesting I take a leaf out her book and be more like her.

I didn't mince my words on that suggestion and almost talked myself into trouble, it was a good job that this had taken place a couple of weeks before the stocktake and my subsequent going on the sick. Once my sick note expired I had two weeks to get through before I had a week's holiday booked, so decided I wasn't going to go back to the doctor and get a new sick note. On my return to work, I was informed that Carol wouldn't be taking any further action against me.

My first day back at work also meant I had to have a 'return to work' interview with the assistant manager; thankfully though it was his day off, so the manager had to do it. After going through the normal routine and the standard questions, she asked how I felt about returning. It was my chance to be brutally honest. The manager, I knew, was not a fan of the night supervisor, indeed she was trying to find ways to get rid of her, but was massively hindered by her assistant manager.

'I used to love my job, now I hate it, I can't stand working with that lazy woman, I do the work and she gets the praise and credit. She's already turned about half of my team against me, and no doubt whilst I've been off she will have turned the rest of them against me, she's poison and I can't work with her, but what choice do I have?' I went on, 'When it's a small delivery she does nothing, she says she is just going to do her admin and paperwork, and that's the last anyone sees of her for that shift. When it's a big delivery and it's all hands to the pump to try and get finished, she does half an hour, then goes missing for an hour, and repeats it all shift. If it's a normal delivery that just requires the attention of both of us for a couple of hours, she chooses the easiest area of work for herself, and takes all shift to finish an hour's work, and even then sometimes we have to bail her out and finish it for her.'

The manager didn't look in the slightest bit shocked or surprised by what I had said. 'This week I don't want you working the delivery with your team, I have some special jobs for you and regardless of how they are coping with the delivery, I need you not to divert from this project.'

I was to work on implementing some new range layouts, and doing some moves to fixturing to accommodate the new layouts. This cheered me up no end; it took care of one of the two weeks before my holiday, and I could worry about the other week later.

A couple of days later, my mother was out of hospital and back at home. I couldn't keep an eye on her though, I lived too far away now, but she did have some home help and for now at least, she had no way of getting her hands on any alcohol, and I was enjoying doing the new layouts and moves at work. That evening at work, the manager had stayed late to see me.

'How would you feel about moving onto the morning team as supervisor? It would mean you'd lose your unsocial pay though?'

I didn't even blink. 'Yes,' I said. Smiling, I continued, 'It would get me away from her.'

'Great, I thought it would appeal to you; you'd be responsible for the filling operation from the warehouse instead of the delivery, and you'll also be responsible for the promotion changeovers.'

'That's fine,' I replied.

'Good, and we would need you to cover holidays on evenings when the supervisor's on holiday, but you'll be fine, as you won't need to work alongside her any more,' the manager told me.

It was set for me to leave evenings straight after my holiday; however, I only had one week on mornings before I had to cover a week off on evenings, but at least things at work were looking up. I had got the change I needed. Now I could finally sort out my life, and hopefully end the cycle of being happy and being depressed.

Seven

Going out in public

As things started to settle down again, and I settled into my new role on mornings, my thoughts began to turn once again to my urge to dress, my feelings of not actually being male, but still unsure about myself and what to do about it.

I'd got myself some extremely realistic prosthetic breasts, but why? I mean, I couldn't display them to anyone, I had never gone out in public whilst dressed, so what use were they?

The only people who had seen my new chest, so to speak, were my friends in the BDSM world, but those gatherings were always in private, away from the unsuspecting public.

My mother was staying clear of alcohol, work was going very well indeed, even the assistant manager had seen me working in the flesh and apologised for telling me to be more like the night supervisor. I was not depressed, so I started to think about where I could dress that was public, but away from people who might know me.

The internet provided me with the answer. I stumbled across a site that was dedicated to cross-dressers and the like. It had chat rooms, and listed nights out that could be attended, gatherings of like-minded people all dressing together and enjoying a night out.

All I had to do was hone my make-up skills a little, buy an outfit that didn't look too trashy, and find a night out that was reasonably local that I could travel to, yet was far enough away to be clear of anyone who might recognise me. I found the ideal night out, and booked a room online for the Travelodge just a few minutes' walk from where the night out would start.

I was assured by people on the website that the Travelodge was a frequently used place to stop over by people on that night out. It was a monthly night out, and the staff were all quite used to men checking in, then leaving for the entertainment that the night would bring dressed as women.

It was some three weeks away yet, and I was already nervous about it. I spent hours in my room practising eyeshadow application, mascara, eyeliner etc. Try as I might, I just could not get the hang of eyeliner, it smudged, it was patchy in places, it was way too thick in others, I poked my eyeball, it was just pure frustration in a pencil.

My female housemate knew about my dressing, and it was her who came to the rescue and showed me how to apply eyeliner and gave me some tips on eyeshadows, and suddenly my nerves about the night out were easing; in fact, they vanished completely.

My outfit had arrived, bought online. The only time I was brave enough to clothes shop whilst in male attire was at peak gift times, like Christmas and Valentine's. The outfit fitted perfectly, and it neatly packed away into my case, along with some make-up and a wig and there it all stayed until the big day arrived.

I was working that morning, finishing around 1pm, and so from work I had a mini mad dash to get home, get some food into me, get showered and freshly shaved and then get to the train station in time for the 4.30pm train to Leeds. I managed it though, and it was only on the train that I started to think about the night in front of me. Still no sign of any nerves, this was not normal for me; the train was packed, yet I knew no one on the train and nobody knew who I was or what I would be doing later.

It was only a five-minute walk from the station to the Travelodge, and I checked in, still with no sign of the nerves that had always been with me all through my life in whatever I did. The evening started at 7.30pm, and I figured on arriving around 8pm.

It was now 5.30pm and I thought it would take an hour to get ready, so I could maybe grab an hour's sleep seeing as I had been awake since 4am and would be out and about until around 3am. Try as I might though, I could not get to sleep. I was excited, too excited to sleep, so I slowly started to get myself ready, thinking I could spend even more time getting my make-up right.

Finally, I was ready for my first public outing, it was 7.45pm, so I thought I may as well go now as opposed to twiddling my thumbs for fifteen minutes. I left the safety of my room, and all was quiet in the corridor. I made it safely to the lift and got in, and that's when the nerves returned, my legs started to shake, my brow started to perspire and my hands were shaking too.

The lift pinged as it reached ground level and the doors opened. The first thing I recall was the noise from the foyer: there were lots of people in the reception area. I couldn't back out now, so I kept my head down and walked quickly through the crowd and out of the Travelodge.

I made my way with some trepidation to the hotel where the others would be gathering for the start of the night. I didn't really know what to expect on this night out, I mean, I knew there would be lots of males in female clothes, from cross-dressers to transvestites and transsexuals as well as their partners and admirers of 'men in drag'.

I knew a couple of people who would be there, I'd met them in a local pub some months before, when in male clothing. They had come in dressed as female and I had got chatting to them, so I figured when I entered, I would make a beeline for them and settle myself down before mingling with anyone else; I would have someone to chat to and calm my nerves.

On entering, I went straight to the bar. I ordered a drink, and then I looked around the room trying to see the couple I knew. It was absolutely heaving with people, I couldn't see my friends, but looking round the room I saw the wide variety of people there. Some looked amazing and, away from the reason why everyone was assembled there, it would have been hard to decipher if they were male or female, but they were in the minority. Most, although they looked good, were instantly recognisable as men, and some just looked bloody awful: there was one guy who had a full beard whose effort was to put a short dress on over a T-shirt and had jeans and trainers on to complete his attire.

I shouldn't really have knocked what anyone was wearing or how anyone looked; each person was only wearing what they found comfortable, and a few were just so outrageous that they got the attention that they wanted. What it did do though was to completely settle my nerves; I knew I probably didn't look great, far from it, but compared to most I looked quite convincing as a woman.

My friends hadn't yet arrived, so I found a table with a seat that was empty and introduced myself as Kelly and asked if they minded me sitting down. The five that were already sat round the table all said hello and introduced themselves and I got chatting to them about the night, mentioning it was my first time out in public. A couple of that group were in the same boat as me, being 'lambs to the slaughter' and we made a pact to try and remain close to one another, safety in numbers, as it were.

I'd been there about half an hour when my friends finally arrived, I was introduced to lots more people as they had arrived with a large group. It was almost like a flying visit from my friends, as soon we were all on our way to the next venue, a gay bar.

I wasn't nervous anymore, I was fully at ease and felt comfortable. We had a couple of drinks in the gay bar, and moved on again to another LGBT bar. An LGBT bar is a place that is either mostly frequented by lesbians, gays, bi-sexual and transgendered folk or a place that is welcoming of that type of person. After that venue, my friends wanted to venture away from the recognised LGBT area of the city and go to a more mainstream pub. I should have been nervous, but I wasn't, I was actually brimming with confidence and we spent a trouble-free, hassle-free hour or so in mainstream pubs before heading back to the rest of the crowd in the 'safe' area of the city. We spent a couple of hours in a nightclub and moved on again to another nightclub to finish the night.

It was about 2.30am when I got back to the Travelodge after having an amazing eye-opening night. I held my head high as I made my way to my room. I no longer cared what anyone might think, I was buzzing with the success of the evening, and went to sleep extremely happy.

The next morning, I woke up to a bit of a dilemma: I had bright red nails, but no nail polish remover. How could I have forgotten to pack my nail varnish remover? What could I do?

I thought about my options: I could journey home as a male with red nails and look completely out of place, and draw attention to myself, or I could put a brave face on it, wear my outfit from the previous night, and put some make-up on and travel home as a female.

In theory, travelling as a female was the more sensible option, provided I got my make-up right. I knew that in general during the day women wore much less make-up than they would for a night out, but against all of this, I also knew that if I travelled as a female, I would then have to make my way from the train station at York to my house, in broad daylight, hoping that I wouldn't bump into anyone I knew. I knew the chances of that happening were slim, but still, with my life so far, if it wasn't for bad luck, I would have had no luck at all.

As a male, I was a shy and nervous person. With red nails on show, I would be even more reserved and in a state of almost constant panic, so I made the decision to go home as a female and proceeded to get myself ready. As I left the comfort of my room, I took one last look in the mirror to check my make-up. It was on the heavy side, but then I did have some five o'clock shadow to cover up. Overall though, I was happy enough to travel.

As I checked out, the girl on reception was lovely and complimented me on how I looked, and I went for my train. She knew I was a male dressed as a female as she had checked me in the day before. I remembered the golden rule of head up and look ahead, not down, and walked with reasonable confidence to the train station. Nobody took any notice of me, they just went about their business and I made it onto my train with no problems.

The train itself was quite full, but the journey passed quickly and trouble-free, and so it was onto the street outside the station, and then onto the bus and home. The entire trip from station to home went completely trouble-free; I got no weird looks or knowing stares and it felt wonderful to be out in broad daylight as Kelly.

Quite simply, I had to do it more often.

To date, I had not yet done any shopping whilst dressed as Kelly, but I now had the confidence to do it as and when I got the opportunity. I had not been out at night as Kelly in York either, but one thing I did find out about myself from that night out and subsequent daytime travel, was that I was comfortable and happy as Kelly. It felt normal to me, it felt natural, like it was my calling, who I really was and possibly even who I needed to become.

Eight

Breasts

I didn't get the chance to have another night out in Leeds for a long time, but I did go out in York and met up with a couple of friends. It was quite uneventful but another feather in my cap, no trouble, no hassle and the confidence was growing within me.

Another plus for me was my mother staying away from alcohol, it had only been about two months, but the signs were encouraging.

I was just planning my next night in Leeds when I had a week of not feeling too great, not exactly ill, just not feeling right. Something was amiss, I was finding myself short of breath at times and taking a deep breath hurt a little, more worrying though was my chest. Not my chest on the inside, but my chest itself: my breasts, if you can call them that, had swollen and could almost fill an A cup. It was most embarrassing, it was hard to hide at work, though I could have possibly passed them off as 'man boobs'.

It transpired, after visiting the doctor, that I had a chest infection and that was most likely the cause of my breasts swelling, and that a course of antibiotics should cure it. For three weeks, I had a natural cleavage. I felt all kinds of emotions, extreme embarrassment, yet excitement, I could caress my own breasts and feel similar feelings to what I thought a woman would feel when her breasts are caressed and fondled. I couldn't kiss them, but I could hold them.

It felt wonderful, I loved having them, like it was meant to be, that I should have real breasts, for those three weeks I felt more like a woman than I had ever felt before, and it was fantastic to be able to dress knowing that I was no longer totally fake, I enjoyed soaping them in the shower and drying them with a soft towel, but those three weeks soon passed.

Once my infection cleared up, I lost my cleavage. I got depressed again, and this time it was a deep depression, one that I struggled to cope with. For a brief time, I had felt like I was a woman and it felt so natural for me to feel as though I was a woman that I found life very hard to cope with once I had lost what I had. People say it is better to have loved and lost than to never have loved at all, I now fully understood that statement, it summed up my feelings completely and I withdrew into my shell once again. I trawled the internet not really knowing what I was looking for. I was going to work, doing my job and coming home, not really interacting with work colleagues, but just going about my work with a heavy heart and coming home to sulk.

My friends knew something was amiss with me, but I kept quiet, I kept brushing them off saying I was OK, just not jumping for joy whilst deep down my mind was racing so much it was making me ill. Not physically ill, but mentally; I was in a very confused state, I wanted my cleavage back, but I didn't want to be in a position at work that caused me embarrassment,

I wanted to feel like a woman again, but I wasn't sure how to go about it. I had facial hair, not heavy hair, it only really required shaving once or twice a week unless I was dressing. With breasts I couldn't have facial hair, but my skin would never stand up to daily shaving.

I should have hit the internet and researched everything, but I wasn't thinking rationally, my mind was mixed up and I continued in a rut for a few weeks. Finally, I spilled out my heart to my BDSM friends, I did it via a personal blog on the website that we used. It was a cry for help, my plea for someone to help me, guide me, advise me. My closest friend there declared her support for me, saying she would be there for me through thick and thin, whenever I needed someone or when I just wanted a shoulder. Another close friend made some suggestions, and I set up a meeting with her. She was a transsexual who had been through a lot herself and probably understood more about me than I did. Maybe she could offer the advice that I needed, or maybe it would just be a waste of time.

When we met, we chatted for hours and hours. I spilled out my innermost feelings and she listened. She told me how she felt before taking the path she took, and advised me what my options were. She stressed many times that she could not tell me what to do, I had to make that choice, but she gave me lots of invaluable advice, the type of advice that you just couldn't get from the internet. She also told me that should I follow a certain path, then I would have to make changes to my image as much as anything else. Everything she told me made absolutely perfect sense and although it never gave me a clear answer or direction to head in, it gave me enough to go home and seriously think about my life, my future life, and my options.

I trawled the internet for further information, I wanted to know everything about all the options that were open to me, I wanted to decide my future fully armed with knowledge, I needed to know every little detail, every plus, and every minus point against every single option I had.

My depression was gone; I was fully focussed on finding my answers and thinking long and hard about what I was going to do, where I was going with my life, how I would do whatever I decided was my path, how my decision would not only affect me, but also my friends, colleagues and family.

After a week or so thinking and researching, I had a full weekend off work, and I put the entire weekend into sorting out in my mind what I was going to do. I stayed up until my eyes closed because my eyelids didn't have the strength left in them to stay open. When they reopened, I continued where I had fallen asleep until the sleep took over once again. The only times I paused from my thoughts and research was for toilet breaks and food, and finally I found my conclusion, finally I made my choice.

I slept on it overnight, and when I woke up, nothing had caused me to waiver from my chosen direction, and I picked up the phone and called my closest friend.

'Sue,' I spoke with lots of excitement in my voice, 'I've made a decision, I need to become a woman, I have to transition, and I don't know how far along the road I'll get, but I have to try.'

'That's great news, I am here for you if you need me, and if you want any help, just give me a call.'

I wasn't sure how far down that road I would get, but I had to make a start. I had considered my options thoroughly, and the NHS route was not really an option, although I decided I would try and run the route alongside my own, because if I made it far enough along my path, I would need the NHS to step in for hormone treatment and even for surgery if I decided to go that far.

The NHS way would involve seeing a doctor, then a local psychiatrist, then maybe being referred to Leeds Gender Identity Clinic, and a lengthy wait to be seen by their psychiatrist, another possible lengthy wait for a second meeting with their psychiatrist, and then possibly being prescribed hormones, and then yet another wait for breast surgery, and then finally another long wait for full gender reassignment surgery.

The thing with feminising hormones is that the earlier you start with them the more effective they are; the older you are, the less effective they become, and I was now 43, and with the NHS I could be 46 before starting on hormones. I knew I could import hormones, and provided they came from a genuine source I would be getting the real thing, not a substitute or a watered-down version, so that was the route I was going to take, but self-medicating with hormones was potentially very dangerous to health.

The first thing I needed to do was start stockpiling hormones. I had worked out that a one-month supply would cost about £100 including customs duty and Royal Mail handling fee. I worked that out based on the middle level recommended dosage; I knew I would be starting on the lowest level though.

For me to become a woman, albeit a transsexual woman, I had to grow my hair long again, and I had to 'condition' work colleagues and family. I also had to subtly start feminising the way I looked. I also needed to deal with my facial hair; there were methods of hair removal that were permanent: IPL and electrolysis.

At some stage I would have to tell my workplace and my family. A name change via deed poll would also be needed somewhere along the line.

But I now had a clear path to follow. I was at the starting point of my journey towards becoming a woman, towards becoming Lisa.

Nine

Subtle changes, gently does it

Before I could make any subtle changes, I had another night out in Leeds, only this time I dressed on arrival at the Travelodge, and then went straight out clothes shopping whilst the stores were still open.

Shopping for clothes whilst dressed as Kelly was invigorating. I felt totally comfortable looking through the array of tops on the rail, and the skirts too, I could do it at a leisurely pace and amongst other people without constantly looking around to see if anyone was watching me. For the first time, too, I could try clothes on before buying them.

I finally settled on a couple of nice tops and a knee-length skirt. Paying was no longer the embarrassing operation it used to be. As a male I could never look the sales assistant in the eye, now I could, and I wasn't afraid of small talk too, I never disguised my voice, it's quite soft as it is, and the whole shopping experience had been an absolute delight.

The night out itself was uneventful, quite enjoyable and

relaxing with no issues, no hassle, no strange looks from anyone, and again the next day I travelled home as Kelly, only this time it was wholly by choice.

The first of my subtle changes then took place: I started to wear clear nail varnish to work. Nobody said anything about it, at least not to me. I am sure some people noticed, but they either kept their thoughts to themselves or told someone else, but I never heard anything mentioned myself, which I found quite pleasing. I had decided that if anyone noticed too soon for my own comfort and questioned me, I would tell them I had brittle nails and was merely strengthening them.

It was nearly three weeks before anyone said anything to me, and it was the assistant manager, who I was now getting along with much better. Whilst outside the building having a cuppa while the manager, assistant manager, and admin person were smoking, Mark asked me why I was wearing nail varnish. At that stage I wasn't ready to tell them that I liked to wear nail varnish and away from work wore bright colours, it was still too soon for that, so I merely stuck to my plan and told him I was strengthening my nails.

Nothing further was said at that point, but I was now on a timescale. I couldn't carry on with clear varnish for too long before someone commented that my nails must be stronger by now, so why continue? I was now dreading that day arriving, but when it came, I knew I would have to face it head on.

Continuing the subtle changes, I decided on a night in the pub, a pub in York, but dressed fully as a male, only with coloured nail varnish and some eyeliner. I decided on only really having the option of black or purple nails at this stage; I would look very strange with red or pink nails, and the eyeliner had to be applied thinly and not be too bold, enough to been seen, but not over the top.

I caught the bus into the city, as I lived just a little too far for walking. The bus was quite empty and posed no problems, and I had decided on the local LGBT pub for some sort of safety. Entering the pub, I was nice and relaxed, I was completely unaware that inside there was a group of people from my small town that had been my prison, people who knew me, including one of my former bullies. At that moment, I wanted a big hole to appear and swallow me whole. I had come out looking for a quiet, relaxing night which would act as a confidence booster for me, instead I had walked into my worst nightmare. My shock turned to despair when they noticed my purple nails and black eyeliner. The bully of the group came over to me and demanded, 'What's with the nails and the eyeliner? You some kind of queer now or something?'

Quick as flash and without thinking, some words just seemed to spurt from my mouth 'What, this? I'm just showing off my better features. When I go home I can take it all off and I'll still be fairly slim and OK looking. When you go home you'll still be balding, fat and ugly.'

Quite where those words came from I just don't know. Normally in that kind of situation, I would have gone bright red with embarrassment and run outside to escape. I half expected to be flattened by him there and then, but all the remaining people in the group burst out laughing, at him! The other people in the pub, who were close enough to have heard everything, joined in the laughter, and his own group started to ridicule my former bully. He swiftly left the pub followed closely by his mates, still ribbing him.

My heart was pounding, I felt liberated, elated, euphoric and rather pleased with myself. My main worry after that incident was the possibility that anyone of that group could be in a pub where any of my family could be, and they could tell them anything about that night, the fact that they had seen me wearing eyeliner, or nail varnish, or both. Still, there was nothing I could do about it, other than wait and see if I got a call to quiz me; it never came though, much to my relief.

I was still depression-free, my mother was still abstaining from alcohol and work was going very well, I was nearly four weeks into wearing my clear nail varnish, and I had received no further comments about it.

Just around the corner was Hallowe'en. It fell on a Friday night, and that night there was a meeting of my BDSM friends in a York pub for drinks and chat. The same day was also our work charity fundraiser day, and dressing in Hallowe'en costumes was the theme. Somehow, I got myself press-ganged into dressing as a witch.

I made a big point of telling those who twisted my arm to be a witch, that when I do something like that, I don't do it in half measures, and that I would be spending the week practising make-up after work each day. Now my major worry was how to do it well enough to be convincing, but not so well that it made people think it was not the first time I had either dressed or worn make-up.

The only thing I did practise was drawing spiders and cobwebs on my face with liquid eyeliner. Even though I say so myself, I got quite good at drawing spiders on my face, it's not as easy as drawing on paper; try looking in a mirror and drawing something simple on your face and you'll get an idea how hard it really is.

So, I was all set and raring to go, but I was also quite nervous. I would be up at 4am to do my make-up and get dressed before heading to work at 5.15am on a motorbike. If I had an accident or got stopped by the police, it would be embarrassing and humiliating.

The day arrived. I got myself ready, and I was quite impressed with the results of my spider drawing. I set off, avoided any mishaps or police interference, and started work. As usual it was quiet for the first couple of hours. Everyone on my morning team complimented me on how good I looked. Just one comment was unnerving: one of the team said that the make-up was too good for a first attempt and that I was walking far too well in heels.

When other staff arrived for work, I got more of the same, and a few more along the lines of, 'You're walking far too well in those heels,' and 'Wow, you look far better as a woman than you do as a male.'

I was quite certain I had planted some seeds of doubt in some people's minds, some of them must now have been thinking, *Does he dress as a woman a lot?* I thought I did well with my answers to some of the questions I got. I had made a point of telling people I didn't do things in half measures, and that I would be practising make-up; hopefully those answers would keep some people's thoughts at bay, and they would think I was just good at what I did when I put my mind to it.

I survived the rest of my shift and went home happy. I now had a few hours before I would need to get ready for the night in York. It would be my first venture out in York whilst dressed, and on a Friday night; not just any Friday though, the last Friday of the month, and Hallowe'en. The city pubs would be packed, and I would be braving them as Kelly. OK, the first pub would be in a private room, but I had no intention of staying there all night. No, I wanted to get out and move into the mainstream pubs, in with the crowds.

A complete outfit change was needed for the night out. I certainly wasn't going to go out as a witch and draw attention to myself; no, the aim of what I was doing, was to blend in, be part of the crowd, to go about my business unnoticed. I wanted other to people to have no reason to do any more than glance at me in much the same way that folk glance at people before continuing with what they are doing. I wanted to avoid the lingering looks, the looks that say, 'Is it or isn't it?'; the looks that plant self-doubt into the mind; the looks that make you feel self-conscious.

It would also be the first time that my BDSM friends had seen me wearing everyday clothes. They had always seen me in trashy clothes, like leather miniskirts that barely even covered the tops of the stockings I used to wear. This time, though, I was dressing to avoid the unwanted looks from the general public, I was dressing more akin to my age, rather than some teenager going to a rave, which was how I had dressed on my first night out in Leeds.

The prosthetic breasts were gone. On reflection, they were far too large for my body frame; as good and natural as they looked, I needed to look as natural as possible in relation to my body frame, and that included not looking like the model Jordan. I toned everything right down: a padded bra that gave me the sort of chest that suited my body frame, boot-cut jeans, some sensible shoes with a small heel, nothing outrageous, a nice patterned blouse, and a warm knee-length coat. After all, it was the end of October.

By the time I had dillied and dallied, I was running slightly late, so I called a taxi. The taxi driver was lovely, he constantly addressed me as 'miss', and the conversation was nice and friendly. All too soon I was at the pub, and so stepped out into the street. The first thing that struck me was how chilly it had become compared to earlier in the day. I wandered inside and received loads of very positive comments about my 'new look' from my friends. I spent a couple of hours with my friends, my confidence was rocketing by now, and I was keen to move onto a mainstream pub and mingle with the public, so I said my goodbyes and left the relative safety that I had been in and went out into the wide unknown.

I already knew which pub I was going to go to, and my heart was beating so fast that I thought it could burst at any time. Despite being quietly confident, inside, my stomach was doing somersaults and my legs were starting to feel heavy. As I reached the pub, it was plain to see that it was jam-packed with people; too late to back out though, not that I wanted to. I took a deep breath and stepped past the bouncers and inside. I kept my head up and looked towards the bar, making my way there through the crowd. At the bar, I waited to be served; I kept watching the barmen waiting to draw their attention so they could serve me. It didn't take long, and I ordered my drink effortlessly, nobody nearby batted an eyelid, they just carried on with their lives, I paid and moved away from the bar.

This was now the moment of truth, I was in a packed pub, dressed as Kelly, and alone. I didn't have the comfort of having a friend with me to chat to. I had nothing to do other than have my drink and watch people going about their night; if I was going to look out of place, now would be the time it would show. I never noticed a single awkward glance or any lingering looks aimed in my direction, I never overheard any derisory comments either, my nerves and apprehension eased considerably and I relaxed. I was about halfway through my drink when a guy came up to me and started conversation, the usual you'd expect from a guy on his own. 'Hiya, I'm Lee, not seen you in here before.'

'Kelly, I've only recently moved to York, just having a quick one in here before I join my friends,' I responded. I gave myself a 'get out' in case I felt I needed to escape.

'Well, hello Kelly. I only moved to York last year, so I'm still quite new here,' he told me, 'you don't mind me chatting to you, do you?'

'Not at all, it beats standing alone and passes some time. So how have you found York?' I said.

He wasn't that bad-looking, and I'd say about thirty years old. While he certainly wasn't my type, I was happy to have someone to chat to whilst I finished my drink, and so far, he hadn't twigged that he was talking to a man dressed as a woman.

'Yeah, not bad, it's a bit hard making friends though, it's like you see a different crowd every time you go out,' he replied to my question.

'Yes, I know what you mean, but York does get a lot of people from the villages coming for a night out,' I said.

'Don't think I'm being forward or anything, Kelly, but I must say you look lovely.'

'Aww, thank you, that's very kind of you to say, and please don't be offended, but I'm not really into guys in that way. You look nice, but I do tend to go for girls,' I said with a wry smile.

The conversation went on for a few minutes longer, exchanging pleasantries, before I said I really had to get going and hook up with my friends, and I left. I was really buzzing now, I had survived my big test with no problems, I had also survived the rather unexpected test of having a full-on conversation with a guy without him guessing or rumbling me for who I really was. That, for me, was more than enough excitement for the evening, and I headed for the safe haven of the LGBT pub that was just around the corner. The barmaid in there recognised me straight away. I had talked to her quite a lot and she was the barmaid on the night that I wore eyeliner and shot down my former bully in style. She was aware of what I was doing with my life through our conversations and she instantly complimented me on how I looked.

We got talking again, and I told about my night so far, and how it was my first time out in York fully dressed, and I asked her to be brutally honest with me: did I really look OK? She answered with a yes, a little less make-up would be perfect, but otherwise I looked very good. That just rounded off what was a very successful first night out for me, I really was floating around on cloud nine and feeling very satisfied with myself.

Eventually I made my way home, via taxi. The buses had long since stopped running, and again the taxi driver was very polite and courteous. I slept soundly that night, very satisfied with how the entire evening had gone. I could not have wished for it to go any better.

Ten

The next few steps

The intention I had was to take small, baby steps, nothing too drastic too soon, but the way things had gone so far, I now knew that I could probably cope living full-time as female once I had everything in place.

I needed to start on facial hair removal, as this step would take a long time to achieve the results I sought. I also knew that by early to late January I would have stockpiled enough hormones to commence taking them, which would mean booking in to see my doctor for bloods tests and discuss my gender identity issues. This would be the first step on the road to reaching Leeds GIC and onto the NHS system for appraisal and surgery eventually.

The other thing that would also be looming large on the horizon in January would be telling my parents. That was the one thing above all else that I feared. Still, I needed not to worry too much just yet, after all, it was still only the start of November.

I also needed to think about a name: Kelly just didn't sit right for my age group, but I had already decided I would change my surname too, and Kelly could be used for that. I just needed to find the right name that would sit well with Kelly and suit my age. After the previous night, I decided to be Kelly again and head to Leeds for a daytime shopping trip.

The train journey there was a new experience. I had travelled by train during the day before, but today, Leeds United football team were playing at home and it was standing room only on the train. It was packed with Leeds fans. If I could survive this, I could survive anything, and survive it I did; it was very uneventful to say the least. I never noticed any lingering looks nor overheard any adverse comments, and so on arrival in Leeds, I headed for the shops.

I took my time milling around the clothing sections in the shops, not really knowing what I was shopping for, just hoping I would see something and think, *I must get that*. I tried on a variety of things, and it never even occurred to me that other people may be watching, I was just so at ease with myself, I was in my element.

I eventually settled on a couple of tops, and some jeans, which I paid for with no funny looks from the assistant, and I made my way towards a café. I never got there though. I bumped into some friends, and instead we all went to a pub for a pub meal. It was a lovely afternoon, chatting away like there was no tomorrow, and all too soon we realised it was already dark and approaching 8pm.

I caught my train home, and my thoughts began turning towards researching where I could go for facial hair removal, and I was making plans in my head to hit the internet once I got home. As I was walking out of the train station at York, though, one of my worst fears happened: walking towards me was someone from work. I could do absolutely nothing other than continue in the direction I was already travelling in. My head was spinning. I hoped and prayed that he wouldn't recognise me, I kept my eyes fixed on him, he did look straight at me, but it was just a glance.

As we passed he glanced sideways, and then continued into the station, and I carried on with my trip back to my house. I was unsure if I was safe to breathe a huge sigh of relief or not, but I did anyway. At least if he had recognised me, he hadn't stopped me in my tracks at the station, but it was now going to be a long torturous agonising wait until work on Monday morning to find out if I had been rumbled.

I spent all day Sunday worrying about what to say if he had indeed recognised me. I knew I would have to seek a meeting with the manager to outline my plans and intentions if he did know it was me who passed him wearing a dress. It would force my hand, and I felt that in myself I was nowhere near ready for that. I had a restless night's sleep, and felt very apprehensive at work, waiting to find out if anything was mentioned to me about Saturday night and the train station. I had worried and panicked over nothing, though. Nothing was said, not even any whispers. I had got away with it, and the cloud hanging over my head gave way to bright sunshine.

After my shift, I started exploring facial hair removal, and discovered Groupon. I signed up, and the very next day, included amongst the daily offers was one for Intense Pulsed Light hair removal, IPL. I considered the offer; it was a course of six treatments and cost just £59, saving me almost £600. I didn't need to think twice, and grabbed that offer straight away.

I also started looking at a website that listed the most popular girls' names for each year. I looked at the couple of years either side of my birth year and noted down the top ten for each year. I went through the list saying each name aloud and following it with Kelly, I wanted to know how it sounded. Some names I didn't even bother with as I just hated them without having to say them out loud. I really liked about four of the names from the list I had written down, but there was one name that I fell in love with. It sat perfectly with Kelly, it sounded right, and I just couldn't get it out of my head. That name was Lisa. I was now officially on the road to becoming Lisa.

Over the next few days I took stock of where I was, what I had achieved so far, what my goals for the coming couple of months were, and was there anything I needed to change? I wasn't sure if anything really needed changing, but I did then start to write a journal about what I was doing with my life. I only started in order that I could look back and see how far I had progressed, or how much I had changed, so I could see any errors I may have made, or even just see where I had gone wrong. I wanted to write down all the highs and all the lows. The path I had set out on was a long one, full of ups and downs, and I suppose in times of feeling low, I also wanted to be able to read through my high points if only to cheer myself up, or just to motivate me into continuing onwards, through thick and thin.

I wrote about what I was I doing on the BDSM website in the form a personal blog. I never looked for any response from anyone, but I was blown away with all the messages of support I got, and not just from people I knew, they were coming in from all over the world, many people saying how brave I was in taking the steps I was taking.

I have never once thought that what I was doing, the path I was walking along, was in any way brave. I only adhered to one thought, which was that I was only doing what I felt I had to do in order to live as happy and as full a life as I could.

Within a couple of days, my Groupon voucher for my IPL was ready for me to print out and present to the beautician. I made an appointment for what they call a patch test, before the real treatment could begin. IPL is not suitable for all skin types, but I was OK, and booked my first session for the following week.

By now it was mid-November and some of the staff at work were already getting on my case about dressing up again; this time they were provoking me into dressing as Mrs Santa for the Christmas charity fundraiser. I was standing firm this time, I may have given too much away last time, and I certainly didn't want to add any further weight to what anyone may have already been thinking. I was aiming to slowly conditioning people so that when the time came to inform everyone that I was changing my gender, it would not be the almighty shock that it could be if I just came straight out and told them. That would certainly be a bolt out of the blue; no, I had to carry on with my softly, softly approach.

There was only one person at work whom I could consider calling a true friend. We always flirted outrageously with each other, but only in fun; mind you, it constantly had everyone else thinking we were having an affair. In Sarah, I knew I had someone I could confide in, but I was too scared to let her in on my secret life. We happened to be doing the banking one day and as usual we were chatting away whilst doing it, and somehow the subject of transvestites cropped up. Sarah mentioned that she was watching a series on television called *Ladyboys*, and that she loved seeing men dressing as women; the conversation that followed went something like this:

'Funny you should mention that but…' I stopped in mid-sentence; I had started talking before my brain had caught up, and instantly hoped that I could now move the subject onto something else.

Sarah said, 'But what? There's something you're not telling me, come on you can't stop now, go on, spill the beans.'

'I err… umm, nothing,' I said very nervously and with my face going a lovely shade of crimson. 'I can't say.'

'You've dressed before, haven't you? I thought your make-up was far too good when you were a witch, and you've already told me you keep your legs clean-shaven.'

With my head in my hands I muttered, 'All right, all right, I'll tell you, but you have to promise me you won't tell a soul.'

Sarah, with a wide grin on her face, watched me squirm in my seat. 'Go on, I won't tell anyone, promise.'

I muttered, 'I've been dressing all my life, I'm actually considering changing my gender and transitioning to female.' My heart was now racing, but at the same time it felt like a small weight had been lifted from my shoulders.

'Wow, that explains the nail varnish and growing your hair longer. When are you going to tell everyone? Are you on hormones yet? Now that I know, and looking at you, I can tell – you do look quite feminine.'

'I'll be telling Helen and Mark in January, and that's when I start on hormones… if, and I mean if, I go through with it. I'm stockpiling hormones, but I haven't fully decided yet,' I responded. Helen and Mark were the manager and assistant manager.

'Wow, I'm so happy for you, it's a very brave thing to do, I can't wait to see you as… err, what do you call yourself when you dress?' said Sarah.

'It's not brave, I'm only doing what I need to do to live a happy life. I'm Kelly at the moment, but I will become Lisa when I reach the point where I have to change my name by deed poll, and you might get to see me as Mrs Santa if some of them get their way. They're badgering me into dressing for the Christmas fundraiser. Or I could email a pic to you, see what you think?'

'Tell you what, they all think we are seeing each other anyway, so you dress as Mrs Santa and I'll dress as Mr Santa,' Sarah said.

With that she wrote down her email address, and we finished off doing the banking and somehow, my standing firm and not dressing up for the Christmas fundraiser had fallen apart at the first hurdle. When I got home, I sent a picture via email to Sarah. I didn't put any comments other than 'Guess who?'

I got a reply some half hour later asking who was in the picture; I replied by sending another picture with a comment 'Someone called Kelly…'.

She was very impressed, very complimentary, I was happy.

The very next day, Mark, the assistant manager commented, 'Your hair is getting long, isn't it due for your usual grade two?'

I quickly brushed it off with 'Nah, it's my winter coat.'

The day of my first session of IPL arrived all too quickly. I made a quick escape from work and scooted across to Leeds for my appointment. I had told work that despite it being a promotion change week, I couldn't stay beyond my scheduled finish time as I had an appointment to get to. They did try pressing me about the appointment, but I gave nothing away.

The lady at the salon was lovely, she led me through the procedure and told me what she was doing along every step of the way. Afterwards, she did ask me why, as a male, I wanted my facial hair removing, so I told her about my plans. She wasn't in the slightest bit fazed and even commented that I had a feminine face, and wished me luck.

The session itself was quite intense. A gel is smeared over the area to be targeted, and then you see a flash of bright light, even though you wear protective glasses, followed a split second later by a short jabbing pain. That pain goes away as quickly as it comes, and this is repeated across every area being treated, it can leave your face looking slightly sunburnt for a day or so afterwards too. An appointment was made for the next session, just a few days before Christmas, and then I made my way home.

The following morning at work, Mark saw my face, still a little red, and asked what I'd done to it. I told him that because I have sensitive skin and I get shaving rash every time I shave, I had decided to have some treatment to remove my facial hair.

Word soon got around that I was having some cosmetics done on my face, and later that day I think a conversation was 'set-up' for me because time and time again in the past, whenever someone had suggested I have my legs waxed for the charity we support, I always flatly turned them away.

'Dave, it's a charity fundraiser in a few weeks, do you fancy having your legs waxed?' asked Carol.

'No,' I said firmly, 'there's no point, I don't have much body hair as it is.'

'Aww, go on, it'll be fun, and then your legs will match your face,' said Helen.

'Look, there is no point, I don't have any hair on my legs,' I protested, and instantly realised that I'd said more than I should have.

'You mean you shave your legs?' asked Carol.

'Yes, if you must know I had a problem years ago, which caused me to have hairless patches on my legs, so I shave them all the time now,' I lied.

Then Mark quipped, 'Shaving your legs, getting rid of your facial hair, wearing nail varnish, growing your hair long... Is there something you want to tell us?'

'No,' I snapped back, and walked away in a bit of a huff. I thought that while I had done enough to deflect their little Spanish Inquisition, that I had sown sufficient seeds into their minds.

Over the next couple of weeks, I ventured out, daytimes and evenings, I did clothes shopping, I went into pubs and cafés, and then I decided I had to do my food shopping as Kelly. It's one thing milling around clothes stores and such, it's a different kettle of fish doing the weekly grocery shopping in a supermarket at peak time on a Saturday afternoon. If I could pass this test, then as far dressing was concerned, nothing would faze me; it was my last real hurdle. I was very comfortable and confident going to pubs and doing other shopping, so I tested myself on the last big hurdle from a dressing and 'blending in with the crowd' point of view.

What I was finding hard by now, though, was wearing the wig for any longer than a few hours; my hair was getting long enough to make it very hot, sweaty and uncomfortable. As in all my previous excursions, it passed without any trouble, no strange looks, nothing, and it went as smooth as silk. So far, I just could not believe how well things had progressed, there just had to be some rough times to come, my life does not run smoothly, it never has, so despite everything going like clockwork so far, I still had my apprehension playing ping pong in my mind.

Each time I went out as Kelly, I would start off being nervous, it was like each time was a test, and each time after passing the first couple of people with no problems, my tensions and nerves would vanish. I was now looking forward to the festive season, I was full of hope for the future, and over the past three months I had been happier than at any other time in my life.

Eleven

Trials and tribulations

December started rather quietly. I had a night out in Leeds, but by now I was so comfortable going out as Kelly that it had become quite normal and I was looking forward to Christmas with optimism. Just before that, though, was the rapidly approaching work charity fundraiser.

The day before the fundraiser was my day off, and on the spur of the moment, I went and had my ears pierced; no great big deal there, I went as Dave, I wasn't yet at the point of living as Kelly. By that stage, away from work, I was Kelly only around 25% of the time. The next day, though, I would be at work as Mrs Santa complete with pierced ears. My hair was now long enough to just about cover my ears, so I thought it was probably just about the right time to do it.

I got myself ready, and I must say, I even excelled myself this time. I used some green eyeshadow to draw small Christmas trees on my face, I had metallic green eyeshadow on my eyes, red lipstick of course, and red glitter nail varnish. I got more than a few comments of 'You've done this before,' and 'You're too good in heels.' I had customers commenting on how fantastic my make-up was, some even taking photos.

Nobody noticed my ears, though, that may well have been due the Santa hat I wore, it was slightly too big, so it covered my ears nicely. My ears did get noticed, two days later. It was Mark, as per usual; it was as though absolutely nothing got past him, unless he was sleeping.

'Ah, I see you've got your ears pierced now, are you sure there's something you're not telling us?'

'Like what?' I replied. 'It's only my ears, lots of people have their ears pierced.'

'I know, women have both done, straight men have the left ear done, gay men have the right one done, or both, I ought to know, I am gay,' he informed me.

'Well, I can assure you, I'm not gay, and I know plenty of straight men with both ears done, just like there are lots of men with long hair, and plenty of men who wear nail varnish,' I responded almost snapping my answer, but I got the words out and emphasised them in a way that the conversation ended there.

Christmases gone by had usually been drink-fuelled and reasonably good for me, I wouldn't say I had ever had a great Christmas, but I can say that I had more than my fair share of rubbish ones. Too many Christmases had arrived whilst I was suffering one of my depressions, and as anyone who has suffered from depression will tell you, it's far worse when all those around you are partying and having fun.

This year, though, I was looking forward to a good, possibly even great, Christmas. I was happy, things were going well for me and the future genuinely looked bright. Christmas Day itself was just another day, as it tends to be when you get older and have no children. I opened the presents I had received, and loved every one of them. One of my housemates, Pauline, bought me some lovely girly stuff. I had told her a few months previously what my plans were and her reaction was, 'Fantastic, I'll have a sister to play with!' It was Pauline who had helped me out a bit when I was struggling with eyeliner and eyeshadow combinations.

After cooking and eating dinner (nothing fancy, just a casserole) I settled down to watch some television and while away the time in readiness for the evening. I had been invited round to a friend's house, one of the 'girls' who I met in York and then on my first time out in public in Leeds as Kelly. Another of her friends would also be there, so I got myself ready, put my wig on, and then took it off again. I decided that, as it was just a friend's house and not the pub or anything like that, I could actually do without the wig for once.

I set off on foot; it was about a forty-minute walk to their house through several housing estates. There were plenty of people around, mostly like me, setting off to the pub or a house, or leaving relatives to go home. I made it past them all with no bother; by now I was confident every time I went out as Kelly.

When I got to the house, Gemma and Gina were already there and on the vodka. We chatted a bit then finally Gemma noticed my hair.

'Hey I love your new wig, it looks so realistic, where did you get it?'

'Oh, it was free, from a site called "Grow Your Own",' I joked.

'I've never heard of that site,' replied Gina.

'No, seriously, it is grow your own.' I emphasised what I was saying by tugging my hair.

'Wow, it's grown so quick, it really suits you,' they both said in harmony.

I was quite chuffed with how that conversation went, we all had a good laugh about it, and started playing scrabble: vodka scrabble. Every time you scored less than ten points, you drank a triple vodka, either neat or with coke. Every fifteen minutes we each tossed a coin; heads meant another triple vodka, tails meant you escaped scot-free.

For anyone scoring fifty points or more, the other two had to drink a triple vodka, and at the end of the game, the winner got a triple vodka, the two losers got three triple vodkas!

By the end of the game we had sunk an awful lot of vodka, and I was very drunk. I'm just glad that my fifty-two-point word to end the game also catapulted me from last place to first and saved my legs from having to carry an extra two triple vodkas! I still had to negotiate the walk home on wobbly legs at some ungodly hour of the morning. After an extremely entertaining night I finally set off home at 4am. How I got home is a mystery, how I made it home in heels without falling over or twisting an ankle is an even bigger mystery.

Just after lunchtime on Boxing Day, it was time to play Santa and deliver my presents to my mother and father. I called in on my father first. We exchanged presents and chatted a bit, then watched a bit of TV. Something came on about gay rights, something to do with gay marriage in America, and my father just came out with some of the most disgusting homophobic comments I had ever heard anyone say, and he also included trannies and lesbians in his bile. It really turned my stomach to hear him spout the drivel spewing from his mouth, and to think in just a few weeks' time I would be telling him that I was transgender and would be changing my gender to female, something that I was now seriously dreading having to do.

That kind of knocked the wind out of my sails and, rather subdued, I left and headed round to my mother's flat. My subdued mood quickly turned to despair: my mother was drunk. Seven months of staying sober had gone down the drain, risking her life for the sake of a drink at Christmas. I pleaded with her to stop right there, I begged her, she kept saying in slurred words that she would stop drinking for my birthday in a few days' time. My birthday had been and gone three weeks previously. As much as I tried to get her to understand that it was Boxing Day, she kept mentioning stopping soon for my birthday, and then she started to comment how well John Major was doing now that he was Prime Minister.

'For crying out loud, Mum, it's 2012 not 1992! Stop this drinking, you're killing yourself.'

I poured away what wine I could find, put her present on the table and left. I just couldn't face seeing her like that for any longer than I had to. I got home and sobbed. Why couldn't I just have a normal Christmas where nothing goes wrong and just occasionally something goes so well it turns a good Christmas into a great one?

On that happy note, I really couldn't wait for the next terrible thing to come along and give my shins a good kick, I sat and pondered what life could throw at me next. I never usually made New Year resolutions, but I did that year: I resolved to be single-minded and determined not to let anyone or anything sway me from chasing my desire to become female. If that meant being disowned by either of my parents or family, then so be it. I was determined to do what was right for me for once.

I made myself a list of things I had to do during January. I had to tell my GP that I had gender identity issues, and hopefully get a referral to a local psychiatrist and get a baseline blood test taken. Also on the list of things to do was to tell both my parents about my plans to start taking my hormones, and seek a formal meeting with my bosses at work to tell them that I intend to change my gender to that of female.

What could possibly go wrong? I mentally prepared myself to lose my father, and possibly my mother, though that may be through killing herself with booze. I also half prepared myself for the doctor refusing to refer me, or take a baseline blood test. I checked up via the internet all about work regulations and legislation surrounding transgender people and the rights that they have in preparation for the meeting with my bosses.

At the start of January, I made an appointment to see my doctor, and asked Helen, the manager at work, when she and Mark would both be available for a confidential chat sometime during January. Helen told me that due to holidays it would not be until towards the end of the month, but that she would put it on the calendar for the last week of the month at the latest. She did enquire what it was about, and I said I couldn't tell her yet but that it was a personal issue.

I wanted to tell my parents on a Saturday or a Sunday, so due to my work rota, that would have to wait until the final weekend of the month, or the coming weekend, the first weekend of the year. I plumped for sooner rather than later: the longer I left it the more likely I would be to put it off until later, but before that, I was at the doctor's on the Friday.

At the doctor's, I told my GP that I had I gender identity issues and we had a brief chat about what made me think that I was female. I also told him that I intended to self-medicate with hormones, which he tried to talk me out of and advised against doing. Every doctor in the land will do the same. I said that I had researched the NHS system of going through gender reassignment, and how long I could expect it to take in a best-case scenario, and that I would be happy to follow the NHS route whilst self-medicating rather than doing it all alone. Also, that I would like to be able to have regular blood tests taken if only to ensure I was not damaging my liver or health in any way.

My GP was not sure what to do, or what course of action to take, and so I educated him about what the next steps were: to refer me to a local psychotherapist. He told me that he would have to consult with colleagues and research the whole process surrounding the protocol for GPs dealing with patients with gender identity issues, so he made a new appointment for me, a fortnight later. Strangely, I never felt nervous or tense when telling my doctor about my gender issues, I was calm and collected and fully focussed.

Throughout the following day all I could think about was telling my mother and father the next day, Sunday. I was running every conceivable scenario through my head and how I could react to each possible situation. Part of me was excited, but mostly I was very nervous, apprehensive and tense. With my father, I kind of already knew that what I told him would not go down well. With my mother, I merely hoped first off that she would take in everything and understand what I was saying. If she managed that, then I was hopeful that at least she would be OK with it, and I dared to dream that she would be happy for me.

I was a nervous wreck and didn't sleep at all well. I even took a couple of strong painkillers to try and make me feel drowsy enough to get some decent sleep, even if it was just a few short hours, but no, all night long I was getting an hour or so, then waking up. All told I probably managed about three hours' sleep.

I had told Sue that I was telling my parents on the Sunday, and she sent me a text message wishing me luck just before I set off, and asked me to let her know how it went. I went to my father's house first as he always went out at lunchtime on a Sunday. I had a knot in my stomach as I sat down and took a deep breath, I was so worried and nervous that when I spoke my voice was trembling as much as I was.

'Dad, I have to tell you something about me and what I'm doing with my life, please don't be mad or angry, but I have struggled all my life with an overwhelming feeling that I should have been born a female, and now I am starting to do something about it, I am changing my gender and becoming a woman.'

There was a slight pause, it seemed like an age, but was just a few seconds and then my father exploded into a flurry of verbal abuse, calling me everything from a raving poofter to a tranny. His words were cutting deep into my heart and he continued the barrage of verbal abuse as he moved ever closer to me. I stood up and tried to reason with him, pleading with him to calm down and to listen to me, but the verbal abuse moved up a gear and every other word to come from his mouth was 'fucking'. By now he was pushing me, pushing me closer to the door, and finally shoving me out of it, slamming it shut as soon as I was outside.

I was numb with shock and shaking like a leaf, tears began to well up in my eyes. With heavy legs, I made my way to the riverside and sat on a bench to gather my thoughts and regain my composure. I still had my mother to tell yet.

I sat and I cried. I had tried to set my mind towards the fact that my father would probably disown me, but I never for one moment expected such a torrent of verbal abuse. I was both angry and upset: angry that I had put myself in that position thinking that I probably could have 'conditioned' him over a period of a few months, like I had been doing with my work colleagues, and I was upset that I had been treated like that by my own father. I spent nearly an hour mulling it over and trying to compose myself so that I could go and tell my mother.

I rather sheepishly went to my mother's house. She wasn't exactly sober, and I played holy hell with her before I told her pretty much the same thing that I had told my father, only pausing a lot more and repeating it, adding the odd 'Do you understand, Mum?'

It felt like hard work, but I was nowhere near the bag of nerves that I had been with my father. By the time I left my mother's house, I was quite certain that she had only taken in little snippets of what I had informed her of, and that she didn't really know what I was saying. Deep down, I knew I would have to tell her over and over before it sunk in.

When I finally made it home, it was far later than I had expected to get home and I had quite a few missed calls from Sue together with several text messages. I made a cup of tea and went to my room. I really should have phoned Sue at that point, but I just couldn't face talking to anyone. All I wanted to do was sleep and cry or cry and sleep, I was feeling the same way that I had felt when my best friend took his own life. I was down, depressed and distraught. It was as though I had been told that my father was dead, except he wasn't, he had just forcibly evicted me from his house and had cut me to shreds with his words.

My cup of tea hadn't even cooled enough to sip, never mind drink, when the phone rang again. It was Sue, she was very worried about me by this time, I really tried my best to tell her what had happened, but I couldn't get my words out past my tears, I just cried down the phone for what seemed like ages. I have no idea what garbled words actually came out of my mouth, and although I could hear the words of comfort and support from Sue, they were not registering, not yet. They did later when she called again after my tears had dried up, my eyes were like April showers, dry and then wet, dry and then wet again, each time I thought about what had happened, the tears flowed, and try as I might, I just could not stop thinking about it.

I tried to think of other things, but to no avail. I finally fell asleep through sheer exhaustion, but again I had a broken night's sleep. It was a good job I had a day's holiday from work because I would never have made it through the day without breaking down; when you're extremely tired it's strange how much more emotional you become.

Over the next few days my mood slowly lifted. I was trying to look at the positives in my life, instead of the negatives. By now, away from work, I was living about 80-90% of the time as female, including doing almost all my shopping as Kelly, and I never went to pubs or clubs or any other social outing in male mode anymore. If I couldn't do it as Kelly, I just didn't do it.

I decided to give my father a couple of weeks or so to calm down and maybe digest what I had tried to tell him, and then if he hadn't contacted me, I would maybe try a tentative phone call to test the water. That gave me the hope to carry on without becoming too depressed.

All too quickly I was back at the doctor's. He was much more clued up this time and went through a few details with me, including letting me know he would be referring me to a local psychotherapist for some standard 'assessment' sessions, and depending on the report from the psychotherapist, my doctor would hopefully refer me to Leeds gender clinic.

He also told me that whilst self-medicating was against his professional advice, he would take a baseline blood test, and take blood tests at varying intervals. However, he would only give me figures; it was going to be up to me to decipher the results, meaning I had to take the figures and use the internet to determine whether I was damaging my health or if I needed to adjust my hormone dosage.

He then gave me a full medical, which I certainly didn't expect, and was ever so slightly embarrassed at because essentially, I was dressed as Kelly. I had jeans on, but lots of women wear jeans, and I had a baggy jumper on, but apart from make-up, I was essentially Kelly. Once that was out of the way, I was given a date, three days later, to come back and see the nurse for my bloods to be taken.

Nothing much occurred in the intervening few days, other than thinking of my parents, and soon I was back at the vampire's side having my blood taken. It would be a week or so before I got the figures, but now that the samples had been sucked from my vein by the vampire I could start taking my hormones. I began on the absolute lowest dosage for each type of hormone pill that I was taking. I had checked thoroughly which ones to take, and the recommended dosages for transgender people, as the dose is very different to that of natal women taking them to supplement their natural hormone levels.

I had read many reports on the internet about other people taking their first dose of hormone pills, and how they instantly felt different. When I took my first dose, I felt nothing. It was the third day when I felt somehow slightly different, I couldn't explain it, I couldn't even describe it, but inside I felt like some sort of change was starting.

By now it was the final week of January. Helen asked me if I still wanted that meeting, to which I replied yes, and she said we'd have it sometime during the week when she and Mark both had the same free time available. Monday turned to Tuesday turned to Wednesday, when out of the blue I was called over the tannoy to go to the manager's office. I instantly knew why, and my legs turned to jelly. I had been chatting to Sarah when the tannoy announcement was made, and she also knew what it was for, she giggled as she said, 'Good luck'.

On entering the manager's office, I sat down opposite Helen and Mark, and began to speak.

'There's no easy way for me to say this, so I'll just come straight out with it. All my life I have been suffering what is known as gender dysphoria, and I have commenced taking feminising hormones, with the intention of changing my gender to female at some stage later in the year.'

There was an ominous pause before they both spoke almost in tandem, 'I must say, I'm not surprised, I thought it was something like that.'

And then Helen showed me what she had written in the diary, 'This week, meet with Dave, think it may be something to do with a sex change.'

'Wow,' was all I could manage.

'Why don't you make us all a cuppa, and we can discuss everything,' Helen said.

My legs worked again now, it was a relief to me that they both already had an inkling about my impending gender change, and I went and made the cuppas.

'Right,' I said, 'I'll go into some details. Gender dysphoria is a condition that affects thousands of people, men and women. For me it's an overwhelming feeling that I should have been female, that I am in the wrong body. It's affected me all my life and I suffer bouts of depression which have only been getting progressively worse, and I finally admitted to myself that I was transgender nearly a year ago, last time I was off sick just after the stocktake.'

Mark was making notes as I spoke, and I paused to allow him to catch up.

'Since September you've probably noticed me allowing my feminine side to show, I've been preparing myself to begin the transition towards being female. I couldn't start hormones until I knew my hair would be a reasonable length by the time the hormones altered my body to the point where it became noticeable to others, and everything I've changed physically since then, ears pierced, clear nail varnish etc., has been in preparation and also to condition people, small changes go unnoticed but the subconscious mind picks it up, so hopefully when I tell people it won't be the big shock that it could have been.'

I went on, 'So, anyway, I've been to the doctor and I'm now awaiting an appointment for an assessment so I can be referred to Leeds gender clinic. I have just started taking hormones, and they will change me, physically and mentally. The physical changes, apart from breast growth, will be losing some of my upper body strength and my skin tone will soften and lighten slightly; mentally, I'll be prone to bouts of laughter or tears for no apparent reason, and I could also suffer mood swings.'

Helen chipped in with, 'Typical woman then.'

And I carried on, 'Basically, I'll be forcing a second puberty on myself, and I'm not certain exactly how I'll react to it, it may be too much for me to cope with and cause me to stop everything, but that's just a slim possibility. On the physical side, hormones affect everyone differently and at different rates. I could develop quickly or be very slow. I could reach the point of having to tell staff within a couple of months if I develop quickly, but more likely I would imagine it'd be about six to nine months before I need to tell people.'

By now I had no nerves whatsoever and was in my element. 'At some stage, so that I can start to live my life fully as female, I must change my name by deed poll, and when that is done, then I would be working here as a female too.'

Helen asked, 'So do you know what sort of timescale we are looking at?'

'Well, I can't give a definite timescale yet, as I just don't know how quickly the hormones will affect me. I would envisage commencing as female here in about six months or so, possibly straight after my holiday in August, so that I have a two-week break from finishing as male and starting as female, and telling the staff about four to six weeks prior to that to give them chance to raise any issues they might have, but obviously I'll monitor my own progress and keep you informed if I need to adjust any timetables.'

Mark jumped in by asking, 'What about toilet facilities?'

'Legally, once I have changed my name and I am living and working as a female, then I am entitled to be treated in the same way as any other female, and that includes the use of female facilities, and it would be discrimination against me if I was not permitted to use the female toilets.'

Over the next twenty minutes or so we went through various details, what things entailed, what I needed my bosses to do, what they required me to do and I answered some of their questions. Helen then asked how often I dressed as a woman, and I answered, 'Away from work I live about 90% of my life as female.'

Mark then asked, 'So does that mean you go out to pubs and stuff as a woman?'

'Yes,' I responded, 'I don't do anything as a male apart from visit the bank or when I go to the garage.'

Mark followed up with, 'Don't you worry about bumping into people from work when you're out?'

'Well, it's funny you should ask that,' I started, 'there was one night when I was just coming back from Leeds and was leaving York station, and someone from work was just going into the station, and we passed each other literally just a couple of feet apart, and they never recognised me,' I grinned.

Helen jumped in, 'Blimey, who was it?'

I tried my hardest not to laugh when I said, 'It was Mark.'

He was completely gobsmacked so I added, 'But back in November I was still wearing a wig.'

With that we ended the meeting and I was reassured that all aspects of the meeting would remain confidential, and I was reminded to follow up the meeting with a letter confirming what I'd talked about and including a rough timescale.

Well, I left the office with a spring in my step and went straight to Sarah and told her how it had gone, including the part about Mark being gobsmacked when I told him he had walked straight past me.

The next day someone else commented on my weight, 'You look like you've lost loads of weight, how have you done it? You look good for it.'

I responded with, 'I don't know, I haven't dieted so it must have just come off.'

Later I checked my weight and had indeed lost weight; I was now down to just over ten stone.

Twelve

A feather in my cap

After the breakneck speed of events in January, February was quiet in comparison. I was on tenterhooks waiting for an appointment with the psychotherapist, I hadn't heard anything from my father, and I am ashamed to say that I left it at that. I was actually too scared to attempt any sort of contact, I feared rejection, being hurt mentally and I suppose the thing that would hurt me most would be my father just rejecting the phone call without even answering it. Deep down I was just living in the hope that he would contact me.

Work-wise, everything was going smoothly. I wrote my letter confirming the details of my discussion with the manager and assistant manager, and I followed it with a more detailed timescale of events. I requested a late start on my first day as a female, so that I would be starting when other members of management were already in the building.

I also asked that I be the one who informs the staff, and that it be done around six weeks from my final day as a male worker;

also, I requested to tell the staff from supervisor level upwards around four weeks before the remaining staff, so that they would be prepared and able to field questions from their teams.

In late February I went away to some cottages near Whitby with some of my BDSM friends. I was able to spend the entire weekend as Kelly, or rather as Lisa, and be free from any work or family worries. It was a fabulous weekend and thankfully the weather stayed fair for us. Considering the British winter that we were struggling to escape from, this was a lovely surprise. It meant I could have a wander down the country roads and into Robin Hood's Bay; I loved the freedom of just wandering around the streets and milling around the quaint little souvenir shops. It was thoroughly enjoyable in the weak sunshine of mid-February and I had a very pleasant outdoor coffee and sandwich at a clifftop café overlooking the bay.

By now the hormones were starting to have an effect. I had already radically altered my eating habits, turning more and more to healthier food. I was starting to have mood swings and was becoming tearful or laughing wildly at little things and physically, only a few weeks in, my nipples were extremely sore and my breasts had already increased in size, if only slightly. I was no longer waking up with an erection, something men will understand – commonly known as 'morning glory'.

Back at work after my mini break, I was greeted with the news that our company didn't yet have its own policy on gender, and HR at head office had asked if I would be willing to help them develop the company policy on all things to do with gender, and specifically gender reassignment. To me that was something of a bolt from the blue, but very nice indeed, a feather in my cap, if you like. They had already done the first draft and I had a copy which didn't take me long find a few faults with. I made some alterations and highlighted them, sending them back to HR to look at and waited for the next draft to reach me.

The end of February came and still no sign of an appointment with the psychotherapist. It was now starting to play on mind a little, as with the delays that I knew were to come once I got my referral to Leeds, this was just another thing slowing me down.

The first week of March saw a major revamp at work for the home living section, a complete new look to the department, and that meant working through the night. The team for that was led by me and a few team members from each team, including Sarah, so at least I would have a real friend in amongst the mix of people. It also meant working in casual clothing, and that raised a new worry for me, as by that stage I no longer had any casual male clothing left. I had kept a few things in case of emergency, but nothing that could be worn for work, so I had to wear a pair of my ladies' jeans and a baggy jumper.

The first couple of nights went quietly, but then I had the lighting canopy to do, which meant assembling the display lights and that was an extremely fiddly job. To assemble the chandeliers, each individual droplet had to be put on and the wire was strong but very thin, and it took less than an hour to break every nail on my right hand.

At this stage of my progress my hormones were playing havoc with me. It was all new to me and I hadn't yet learned how to cope with the feelings I had. The light fittings were getting to be more and more frustrating and I was starting to get extremely agitated. I was sat on the floor trying to attach some droplets to a fitting and I was quite close to just breaking down in tears. It was a strange feeling that I didn't know how to handle; prior to taking hormones I would have just knuckled down and got on with it, but here I was, sat on the floor almost crying just because some little droplet didn't want to be attached to the light fitting that I was assembling.

Sarah could see I was getting upset and suggested I go and get a glass of water and take a breather, which I did, and boy was I glad I did. No sooner had I got out of sight of the rest of the staff, I started to cry. Once I pulled myself together I carried on with the job in hand; thankfully, that was the only incident of the week, and soon the whole revamp was completed.

That weekend it was my father's birthday. I still had not had any contact with him, so I decided to make the first move. I got a card and underneath a teabag I put a folded-up ten-pound note. Below that, I put the usual message that I put in birthday cards to my father: 'Have a drink on me.' I decided I would attempt to deliver it in person. If he shut the door on me, then at least I would know exactly where I stood.

I set off with butterflies in my stomach, my apprehension only increasing as I got closer and closer to my father's house. By the time I pulled up outside his home I was a complete bag of nerves. Within a few moments, I would either be completely rejected and without a father, or I would still have something to work on to keep my father. I knocked on the door, only my knees were knocking louder, and waited, and waited, but nothing.

Maybe he was in the shower, or hadn't heard me knocking. I knocked again and waited, this waiting was doing absolutely nothing to ease my nerves, in fact they only got worse, and the only thing to ease them was the eventual realisation that he was not at home. I posted the card through the letterbox and went home. Now I wouldn't know anything until he either made contact, or I heard nothing at all, in which case I would then know that he'd put me out of his mind and had no father left.

The wait was killing me and I had only been home a couple of hours; talk about being impatient. Before long, the weekend had passed and I still had not heard anything. I was feeling down, very down. I feared that I had lost my father and I didn't know how to put the feeling of rejection to the back of my mind.

I struggled to concentrate at work; by the time Tuesday arrived, I was virtually distraught.

I muddled my way through, but my mind was elsewhere, I had told Sue about going to hand deliver my father's card, and that I ended up having to post it through the letterbox. I was very tearful when I told her that I still hadn't heard from my father. I had concluded that he must have just thrown the card in the bin, and I was now beginning the process of coming to terms with the fact that I no longer had a father; I was grieving.

Then next day, at home, I watched TV and played games on my PC, I was doing whatever I could to not think about anything at all, and then the phone rang.

'Are you working this weekend?' It was my father.

'No, why?' I asked tentatively.

'I think you should come through then, and we can have a chat,' responded my father.

'OK, great, Sunday is probably best for me, what time?' I replied.

'Any time before twelve, just give me a call when you are setting off.'

'Right, OK then, I will, see you Sunday,' and the conversation ended there.

There was no hint of what he wanted to talk about; it did get me slightly worried to begin with, but the more I thought about it, the more I began to think why would he want a one-to-one chat if it was to tell me I was being cut out of his life completely? I figured at worst he wanted a few more details to make up his mind about what to do: support me, refuse to acknowledge me as a female or to disown me.

Thoughts of Sunday dominated my mind, my thoughts, and my dreams for the rest of the week. I went through all kinds of scenarios in my head and by the time Sunday arrived I was cautiously optimistic but also wary that my conclusions could be way off the mark. I didn't sleep well the night before and was up and about way too early, and it only gave me yet more time to dwell on my thoughts. Time passed so slowly that morning, but eventually I was ready to set off, and I gave my father a call to let him know I was on my way.

On arrival, I was greeted by a cup of tea already made and waiting. I sat down and waited, I wanted my father to open the conversation. There was an eerie silence which seemed to last forever, but it was finally broken when my father spoke.

'I'd like some more details, why? Why now? What's involved?' he asked.

'Well, I'm doing it because doing nothing about it only means I'll continue to suffer bouts of depression and each time it gets worse and takes longer to come out of. It's because I have an overwhelming feeling that I should have been born female, there's nothing I can do to change that. I don't want to be transgender, I wish I wasn't, but I am. If I'd had the internet twenty years ago, I would have realised I was not alone in being transgender, but I didn't and I just thought I was some sort of freak, a weirdo or something, so I hid it behind girlfriends and even got married to help hide what I was.'

I paused for breath, and then continued to tell him the route I was taking, and that I was already on hormones and changes were already taking place. I told him about my timetable of events, and that he wouldn't be losing me, just that I would no longer be his son, but would be 'almost' the daughter that he had always wanted.

'Well, I have done some research myself, and I am sorry for the way I reacted when you told me, you caught me off guard and I reacted badly, I know I sometimes come across as set in my ways and old-fashioned, but with the research I did, and what you've told me, I am happy for you, really I am, and you've got my support'.

Gosh, was this really my father? He was completely different to everything I had come to know about him, I did wonder if he had been abducted by aliens and replaced by an android, this was certainly not the man I knew to be my father. We chatted for a good couple of hours, I showed him a couple of pictures of me as Lisa, and he was mightily impressed and relieved that he could now get a picture of Lily Savage or Eddie Izzard out of his head.

We made plans to have a night out in York, no date set, just playing it by ear as to a date that suited us both. He wanted to see Lisa in the flesh and was taking interest in what I was doing with my life. He asked me to keep him informed of my progress and his personality was so far from what I had known, that I really did start to believe he had been replaced by an android, or that he'd taken a bang on the head. It just wasn't him, but hell, compared to the old him, I would take this new version any day.

A massive weight had suddenly lifted from my shoulders. I felt like I had won the lottery, I couldn't stop smiling and the tears started to well up in my eyes, I just couldn't hold myself together, and tears of joy began to roll down my face.

'Typical woman,' was my father's comment as he came across and gave me a big hug.

'I can't help it,' I managed to mumble through the tears, 'I thought that I'd lost you.'

'You're my son… sorry, daughter, I would never throw you out of my life; just don't ever spring something on me like you did, it was a shock and hard to take in, and be careful with the hormones, and keep getting your blood things checked.'

'Blood tests, Dad,' I managed in a sniffle, 'liver function and testosterone levels, plus some others.'

Time flew past and all too soon it was time for me and my father to go out. I joined him at the pub for a quick drink, nonalcoholic as I was on the motorbike, and we chatted some more, but not on the subject of me, just general everyday chit-chat. I wasn't ready for people to listen in on any conversation about me becoming female. It was a very pleasant drink, but I had other things still do, so I bade my farewells and moved across town to my mother's flat. I decided on the spur of the moment to check in on Mum and have another go at getting her to understand my life changes.

Again, she wasn't exactly *compos mentis*, not inebriated but certainly not sober, and I knew straight away I would have my work cut out to get through to her. Her drinking was driving me to despair, she was slowly killing herself, and nothing I or anyone else could say was reaching through the alcohol barrier that stood between real life and the drunken haze that she seemed to be semi-permanently in.

I tried my best to reach out to her, to get her to repeat what I was telling her about my ever-changing life, but as much as she could repeat my words, she wasn't taking it in and remembering it. I didn't stay too long, it had been an extremely emotional roller coaster of a day for me, I had the euphoria of having my father back in my life and fully supportive, and had followed it with a dive into the pits of gloom with my mother and her marriage to alcohol.

Once I got home, I reflected on the day. I didn't dwell on my mother, I was fast losing the will to live where she was concerned, but my thoughts were completely dominated by the time I had spent with my father, and again, I'm not ashamed to admit that I sat and wept tears of sheer joy and happiness. My mother apart, my life was on the up and I was looking forward to the future; it actually looked like a bright future for once in my life.

I had a spring in my step now, and I started looking up information on the internet in readiness for my name change.

I found a site that had very simple, easy-to-follow instructions and you could fill in the forms online too. At that time, I didn't have a date in my mind for my name change to take effect, but with this one you could leave the date blank, so I went ahead and filled it in, new name Lisa Kelly, and then moved onto the final page to pay for it.

I decided to get it all done and paid for there and then whilst I had the money. With my life and knowing my luck, something would crop up and leave me without the funds to pay for my deed poll when the time came to get it all completed. All I had to do now was wait for it to be delivered, and then when the time came, fill in the appropriate details and have it witnessed, much like a driving licence, add the date, and then post it back. It would then be just a couple of days before I would have the legal name change deed poll in my hands ready to send off around the country to all the parties who needed to know my new details. That was for the future, though; the here and now was just as important and more preparation was still needed.

Thirteen

Psychotherapy

A week or so after regaining my father, I was still high up on cloud nine. I was in the staff room at work and just one other person was in there, and I started muttering to myself. It was barely audible but I was muttering about the need to pass my driving test, hopefully by the time I had my two weeks' holiday in August, and about being jubilant over my father, and that I could see my father as Lisa, yes, Lisa: my father never knew or met me as Kelly and I had told him about my name change to Lisa.

When I looked up after making a cup of tea whilst mumbling away to myself, I noticed the other person in the staff room looking at me in a rather strange way. And then it dawned on me that just possibly, she may have overhead my ramblings and I instantly thought, *Oh bugger, me and my big mouth, I hope she never heard me.*

I was just a little bit too wary of asking her why she was looking at me in the way she was in case I ended up with an awkward question to answer, so I merely forced a smile, said good morning and started whistling 'Rudolph the Red-Nosed Reindeer' as I left the room. Yes, Rudolph in March!

My work colleagues are used to me whistling tunes that are out of season, and saying good morning no matter what time of day it is, it's just one of my strange quirks that helps keep a smile on my face, and sometimes brings a smile to others too. The music at work is on a three-hour loop, so during a shift I hear some songs three times a day, and it's very repetitive and monotonous when it's the same songs at the same time each day, and thus, I could often be heard singing along to the songs, but using different words.

The next day Sarah told me that Mandy had asked her a question about me; seeing as she knew that we were close friends, she'd asked Sarah if I was having a sex change. Sarah said she would be best asking me; although she didn't keep secrets from Mandy, she also didn't want to break my trust.

Mandy's next shift was the following day, so when she arrived at work, rather than allow her to stew over how best to approach me, I went to her and asked if I could have a quick word. We went somewhere private and I told her that Sarah had 'pre-warned' me, and so I decided to tell her everything.

'To answer the question that you asked Sarah, yes, I am changing my gender. I suffer from depression brought on by gender dysphoria and these depressions are only getting worse, so I made the decision to follow my inner feelings that I am in fact female, just in the body of a male. I'm already on hormones and planning to inform the staff in a couple of months, the plan being that I finish as Dave when my August holiday starts and when I return from that I will be Lisa. So please, do not tell anyone; if word gets out too soon it would hinder everything I am working towards and make my work life awkward.'

Mandy replied, 'Wow, I am happy for you, it's very brave of you and I won't tell a soul.'

'Oh, I'm not brave, I'm just doing what I have to do in order be happy in my life. If you've got any questions, don't hesitate to ask me, I'll answer as best as I can, but how did you guess? Was it me muttering away to myself in the staff room yesterday?'

'Well, that just finished off what I had kind of guessed. I mean, you wear nail varnish, have long hair, pierced ears and a few things you do are what women do, not men, so it made me wonder.'

I laughed and said, 'Yes, I do tend to act like a woman a lot, but when I had really short hair nobody ever seemed to notice. Thanks for keeping this a secret for me.'

Apart from Mandy, I also heard that one or two were starting to talk amongst themselves and speculating about me due to the changes that I had made over the past few months. My softly, softly approach appeared to be having the desired effect of conditioning peoples' minds.

Shortly after that incident I had the first of my psychotherapy sessions that would ultimately determine whether I would get the referral to Leeds GIC that I was seeking. I had to attend straight from work which meant attending as Dave rather than my preference of being Lisa away from work. Naturally enough I was quite nervous; I had no idea what sort of questions to expect although I did know there would be some personal questions. It turned out that I had no reason to be nervous; the first session was basic with soft questions about how I feel and how I saw myself and the future. I was quite relieved that I had breezed through the first one with no problems and a date was set for my next session. Next time I would be able to attend as Lisa as it was my day off from work.

Life was mundane for the next week with nothing much going on until the day of my second therapy session. I got myself ready in very good time and caught a bus into the city. I had plenty of time before my appointment, so I perused a few shops, window shopping mostly but I did find a nice pair of shoes, so I made a mental note to call in on my way back from my session. The place in which I would be grilled was about a mile, maybe a mile and half out of the centre and as it was a reasonably nice day, I decided to walk.

For a weekday, there was a surprising number of people around shopping and treading the streets but by now I was perfectly happy wandering amongst the crowds and at one point I even passed one of the guys from work. Nerves took over for a few anxious moments but the fear of being recognised and having my secret revealed passed without hitch, he looked straight at me and completely failed to recognise me.

At the psychotherapy session, I soon found out that I was to talk about my childhood and early adulthood. I got quite upset and tearful when recalling my bullying, I was pretty upset by the end of the session and I never even mentioned being raped when I was just nineteen, I was just too upset and rather embarrassed. I was quizzed about my sex life and my leanings and experiences, and again I felt a little uncomfortable talking to a stranger about this but I muddled through. I couldn't grasp why my sex life or indeed my sexual orientation was being discussed, I felt it had no bearing on my feelings of being a female in a male body. I found that session to be a rather humbling and humiliating occasion.

By the end, my therapist could see that I was visibly shaken and a little upset with myself, and so I had a cup of tea in the waiting room whilst I pulled myself together for the walk back to the bus station.

A few days later I had my final session, with yet more soul-searching questions and answers. By now though I knew what to expect and I sailed through with ease. I was comfortable answering these questions now. Yes, I got a little emotional at times, but I could feel inside that I was getting somewhere. It was almost as if putting myself through all this soul-searching and heart-wrenching recollections of my past life were part of the process towards a kind of mental healing that would maybe lead me onto the thing I desired: becoming a woman, becoming Lisa.

Once the session was over, my therapist could finally speak freely and made a point of telling me that the way I looked when I attended as Lisa and the way in which I carried myself combined with my conservative use of make-up meant that I could easily blend in with everyday people going about their lives with no concerns, and that should I follow through with everything and live full-time as Lisa then she could see no reason why I could not lead a happy life without any problems.

I did thank her for her comments; she didn't have to remark on my ability to be the person I wanted to be, she did not even have to comment on anything about me. I then asked what happened from here, to which she told me that she would be instructing my GP to refer me to Leeds Gender Identity Clinic but, there was always a but, although it was now only the end of April, the list for this year was full and I would not be seen until the next financial year started, next April! Normally news like this would have got me feeling down in the dumps; however I was elated at getting past the first hurdle on the real road towards prescribed hormones and surgery.

Once I got home I began to research again what the NHS route would expect me to do; each time I researched, nothing had changed, but I wanted to make sure and I would research it all time and time again over the coming months. I found out that if I happened to be married then I would be expected to divorce to continue along the road to becoming a woman; there was no reason why someone couldn't live together in a civil partnership, but any marriage would have to be dissolved. Thankfully, that didn't apply to me as I was young, free and single; well, free and single, not quite so sure about the young part.

I would be expected to change my name by deed poll and commence living full-time as a female. Well, I would be doing that long before even reaching my first consultation, and I would be able to provide documented proof.

After two or three more consultations, you are accepted on to the care pathway; then, hormones may be prescribed for a trial period and if there were no bad reactions, hormones would be prescribed continually, and then breast augmentation surgery could happen around twelve to eighteen months later, depending on hormone levels being within preset limits for surgery.

What I hadn't planned was that during my wait for a first appraisal appointment, the protocol would change to an interim protocol, and that interim protocol no longer provided breast augmentation surgery for transgender people.

With luck my hormone levels would already be close to those surgery limits by the time I reached my first consultation, although I would need to be prescribed hormones and my levels monitored for a period. I did very much hope that my year or so self-medicating would reduce my own time spent waiting for surgery.

Fourteen

Coming out at work

And so it was headlong straight into my next hurdle: work was becoming far too painful using cling film to bind my chest. There was a heatwave kicking in and within just a couple of hours of my shift each day, I was becoming sweaty due to the binding and getting tetchy due to the tenderness of my nipples rubbing against wet cling film. Quite simply, I had to be more comfortable whilst working and that would mean telling all the staff about my gender change sooner than planned.

Stopping me at that moment was the small matter of the inter-store spring competition. Basically, all stores were judged on presentation, standards, promotion features to company standard and overall 'customer' impression. The first round is always against stores in our own region, with the winner going forward to be judged against other regional winners that are put into two groups, northern stores and southern stores, and then the winner of each section is pitted against each other to find the best in the whole company.

Winning the region is an excellent standard, reaching the overall final is a real achievement. Whilst we were still in the competition, all the focus would be on the competition itself and that would mean having to delay telling the staff. The process involved our store being judged to find the regional winner during the first week of May. Victory would mean being judged for the northern title in the second week of May and the overall company winner being judged in the third week of May and immediately after that we would be into a bank holiday week and just too busy to take time out to tell the staff, so I was potentially looking at June at the earliest if we went all the way in the inter-store competition.

Our manager certainly didn't want the extra workload involved in getting the store up to competition-winning standard; we had been there just six months earlier with the Christmas competition. As luck would have it, well, luck for me and being able to inform the staff, just over a week before judging in the first round, our evening delivery of stock from the distribution centre got severely delayed and arrived an hour before the delivery staff were due to lock up and go home. This meant that the following morning, on top of a large promotion change to complete before we opened, there was also a full delivery of stock that needed to be put onto the shelves.

Now, before any competition between stores, the customer comes first, so I took the decision to put some people onto working through the delivery and two people onto changing the five-metre promotion that had to be changed that day. Whilst doing this, it also meant that the store itself looked untidy due to the empty promotion shelves and several cages of stock on the shop floor, making customer navigation a little bit more difficult.

Sheer misfortune struck next, we had a surprise unannounced visit from head office. When they visit, they always report back from a customer perspective as well as from their own perspective. As you can imagine, we got a scathing report from them, it was so hot you could have fried an egg on it... to say we got slated was a gross understatement. It mattered not one bit to them that transport had yet again badly let us down and left us with no chance to get the delivery stock onto the shelves. It didn't matter to them that every single day that week the delivery arrived at least two hours late and the whole week had been spent playing catch-up with the delivery at the expense of getting the promotion implemented. The net result was that our regional manager gave us the option to pull out of the inter-store competition, an option our store manager jumped at, and that also meant that I would be free to inform the staff the following week and the date was set for the Monday.

It got to the Saturday beforehand and I wasn't the least bit nervous. The manager then told me that Monday would be far too busy and in order to catch as many staff in work on the same day he suggested Wednesday instead. I can't explain why, but suddenly the nerves kicked in and I started to think about exactly what I would say. I knew that come Wednesday I would only have around fifteen minutes with each group of staff and getting in enough detail in that time without confusing anyone would be tricky.

I made quite a few rough drafts of what to say, but each one sounded awful when I read them out aloud, and they all ended up in the bin. Then I hit on the idea of bullet-pointing the major information and giving a very brief snippet of information on each point. Once I had finished I read it out loud to myself and it sounded OK, it gave me a base to work on and improve.

All my nerves vanished once again and I slept quite soundly until Tuesday night when my attempts at sleep were constantly interrupted by a dream. All I could dream about was how it would all go horribly wrong when informing the staff and it all led to a very unsettled and pretty much sleepless night. The following morning I woke up feeling more tired than when I went to sleep as well as being a complete nervous wreck and my later start time, some three hours later than normal, left me with even more time to contemplate the nature of the day ahead of me.

I arrived at work just before my start time and the intention was for Chris, our new assistant manager who had already been briefed about me, to deliver his usual daily brief to the staff, only today he would keep it short and then hand over to me.

I put a tannoy out for Helen to contact the admin office as I knew she would be somewhere on the shop floor and finding her could take some time, especially if customers were stopping me to ask where things were.

Helen said, 'Make the cuppas and we'll see you at the staff entrance in a few minutes.'

Helen, Chris and I then went outside so that Helen could have a cigarette and go through the plans for the day. She then commented that I looked like a bag of nerves. I was shaking like a leaf because I knew then that a few minutes later my own morning team would be called in for the daily brief. We finished our cuppas and went back inside. I dashed to the toilet whilst Chris put the tannoy out to summon my team.

Chris read out his daily news and then Helen spoke, 'Dave has got something to tell you all that is very personal to him but before I pass you over to Dave I would like to say that what you are about to be told is confidential and all the staff will be informed during the course of the day so it is imperative that you do not discuss it with other members of staff who may not have been informed. And now it's over to you, Dave.'

I took a deep breath, cleared my throat and for some strange reason I was suddenly very calm and collected, my nerves were gone and I wasn't even shaking like a leaf.

'I've got something rather personal to tell you all, and I wanted to do it in person rather than a letter or via the manager. I've been suffering for a very long time with bouts of depression that have only been getting worse, and the reason behind it all is that have what is known as gender dysphoria. Without going into detail, it basically means I have an overwhelming feeling of being trapped in the wrong body, and for the past eight or nine months I have been preparing myself for changing my gender to that of female. I have two weeks' holiday at the end of August, and when I return in September, I will be returning as female with the name of Lisa Kelly. The reason for telling you this today rather than the planned date of early July is twofold: I have been on female hormones for a while now, and it is becoming increasingly hard for me to hide how these hormones have changed my physical appearance. The methods I have been using make it ever more painful to get through my work, and it's time for me to be able to do my work in relative comfort and less pain. It also gives you all longer to digest everything and ask questions or raise any concerns you might have. I will ask that you keep the questions to a minimum today, as I do have a lot of people to inform, but feel free to ask anything you like. If you would rather ask someone else, the manager and assistant manager will happily answer questions. I'll also ask that today at least, you keep this information to yourselves whilst I see and inform everybody.'

When I stopped talking I waited less than ten seconds for the first question…

'Does that mean you'll start to fancy men?'

'I honestly don't know exactly how the hormones will affect my thinking on that subject, time will tell,' I answered. At that stage I had never revealed to anyone that I was bisexual.

Then it was a flood of people saying things like 'Good for you,' and 'Well done, it's your life and you do look better as a woman,' (they have seen me dressed for charity days) 'You've got the body for it,' 'You've got better legs than me.'

It went down far better than I could ever have dreamed of and it also lifted a huge weight off my shoulders.

The day before all this I had been asked outright by Chloe if I was having a sex change, so I told her everything. Next morning it was agreed that she would inform the till staff who all start at varying intervals and I would try and speak with each of them to answer a few questions as time allowed.

Despite what I was doing, though, I still had my daily duties to do as well, and as the shop floor day staff start at intervals, too, it was decided that I would inform them around 3pm when they would all be in doing their jobs, so I got on with my tasks and for once I was working in comfort. As I knew I would be telling everyone that day I decided to wear a bra for support and comfort and try not to worry about customers noticing some feminine-looking guy with a bra visible underneath a work shirt.

I must admit that on that day I was shying away from customers a little bit to try and avoid them noticing my bra, but I found I was getting through my workload quite easily and making plenty of time to go and talk to the till staff. I kept getting the same recurring comments: 'Do I fancy men now?' 'Wow, that's so brave of you,' 'What made you choose the name Lisa?' and so on.

One of the till team, Val, had a boatload of questions. She wasn't someone who was shy at coming forward so rather than stand and answer questions for twenty minutes I said I would go for my break at the same time as her. During that break the questions ranged from how big will my breasts grow, what will happen to my wedding tackle, will I see you dressed before I go on maternity leave, how long do you have to wait before surgery and quite a few more basic questions, all of which were answered with total honesty.

Around 11am that day our regional manager came for an unannounced visit and that meant Helen had to spend time with him. Without the manager present I could not inform the shop floor team. Time ticked round to 3pm and beyond, soon it was 4.30pm and I was starting to think he'd never leave and began to wonder if I should go into the office and ask if I could 'borrow' my manager for twenty minutes; after all, it was imperative that all staff were informed on the same day to stop any widespread gossip developing. The shop floor team by now knew I had an announcement to make but didn't know what it was about and were constantly fishing for clues but all I could tell them was that I had to wait for Helen.

As 5.30pm rapidly approached and with the shop floor staff leaving at 6pm, I decided I was going to interrupt the regional manager and ask to pinch my manager but just as I approached the office they both emerged. Finally, the regional manager was leaving and I could get on with informing staff. The shop floor team were called up to the office and I went through my speech pretty much using the same words I had used that morning with my own team. Nerves didn't play any part this time as I kind of half expected a similar response to how my own team had taken the news, and so it proved.

The only team left to inform now was my former team on evenings; this was the one that really worried me because the 'bitch from hell' evening supervisor had been so successful in manipulating my own team to turn against me. I really thought if any team would be less than positive it would be them. They had to be done in two groups as half the team started at 6pm and the other half, except one person, started at 7pm.

Strangely the six o'clock starters were the ones who didn't turn against me, but a year had passed since I left the evening team and I couldn't be sure how they would react after the evening supervisor had got her claws into them since then, though I was hopeful this group would at least be reasonable about my news.

Helen and I entered the staff room at six o'clock and Helen made her statement about keeping things confidential and handed over to me. Boy, was I nervous; for the first time since just before telling my own team I was shaking like a leaf and my nervousness came through in my voice too but I got through my speech and anxiously waited for someone to speak. I was praying inside my mind that someone would break the silence and say something positive and the eerie silence lasted for what seemed like an ice age but was more like half a minute.

Have you tried watching thirty seconds tick by whilst desperately waiting for a positive comment? Try it. Honestly, when you are that nervous, those few seconds eat away at you. At last someone spoke.

'Wow, I'm shocked, I thought you were going to tell us that you've got cancer or something, wow.' This was soon followed with 'Good for you,' by another member of staff and then the questions started to flow and the relief on my face must have been clearly visible.

It had been a long and emotionally draining day and I was quite pleased, well, very pleased with how the first evening group had taken the news. Now I had to wait for the next group at seven o'clock, the group I had been dreading all day. As the clock slowly ticked round I was growing ever more anxious; it had been a very tiring day and with the hormones playing havoc with my feelings coupled with how well the day had gone so far, I was getting quite close to tears, not of sadness but tears of sheer, utter relief and joy. But I had one more group ahead of me, the one group that I feared would possibly be troublesome or less than happy for me.

At 7pm Helen and I entered the staff room and by now my stomach was tied up in knots and I felt a little nauseous but there was no way out of telling them about my intentions, so I sat down and waited for Helen to finish addressing the group and then I started.

'I've worked with all of you for several years until last year, so I felt I had to be the one to give you the news I'm about to deliver to you.' I paused for a second to take a breath and attempt to gather myself together, and then continued.

'All my life I have been suffering bouts of depression mainly brought on by what is called gender dysphoria and these depressions have been getting deeper and lasting longer, so much so that I made a decision to radically change my life and stop hiding from my overwhelming feelings that I was born in the wrong body. I am going to be changing my gender later this year to that of female with the name of Lisa. I am already taking female hormones which are changing my body physically and mentally. Mentally, I am prone to bouts of laughter or tears for little or no reason, which I am still learning how to control, the physical changes are softer skin, breast growth and losing some upper body strength and the reason for telling you now rather than closer to my intended start date as Lisa is because the physical changes are making it uncomfortable to work without wearing a bra for support and it also gives you much more time to digest the information and raise any issues with myself or with management.'

I held my breath as I awaited a response, any response. By now I was tired, no, exhausted, so I just wanted to get through the responses or questions quickly and get home.

'One of my friends went from female to male, it's a very brave thing you are doing but you have to do what is right for you.'

Another of the girls followed that with, 'I'm so pleased for you, I hope it all goes well,' and yet more positive comments before one of girls started to cry, which in turn set the other one off and of course I followed suit but I didn't care, it had been a very long hard emotional day and I was euphoric at how the day had panned out with not one bad comment and lots of well wishes and very positive reactions.

There was one person who started at 8pm but Helen was never going to stay much beyond telling the seven o'clock starters so we left the last remaining person in the hands of the evening supervisor and left.

What an amazing day! I could not have wished for it to go any better and a huge weight was lifted from my shoulders. All the major obstacles had been overcome, at least until the time came to inform banks and such of my name change. I felt completely liberated and at ease with myself, at least for the time being.

Fifteen

Girls' night out

A few days after coming out at work, on my day off I met Sarah in the city centre for coffee and had a nice time doing a little bit of shopping. To get into the city centre I caught the bus and it worked out cheaper to buy an all-day ticket rather than a return, which meant I could also hop onto any bus I wanted. To kill two birds with one stone, as I still had some food shopping to do, it was easier to head to the retail park close to work and get my shopping there.

On leaving Sarah, I headed to the retail park and made a last-minute decision to call into work and get a bit of shopping there too; now that all the staff knew about me it felt liberating that I could finally buy odd things from my workplace and take advantage of the staff discount, plus it would give some of the staff the chance to see the real me, Lisa.

I wandered in and said hello to a few of the staff as I got a few bits of shopping, not many of them recognised me at first but all were quite impressed with how I looked. With smug satisfaction I finished my food shopping next door and went home.

Next on my agenda was the long-planned night out with my father. It was about time he met Lisa in the flesh and I arranged to meet him off the bus just outside the cinema. I got there far too early and popped into the nearest pub for some Dutch courage to settle my nerves. I wasn't quite sure how my father would take to Lisa.

Next day would be the York races and some people were already in the city staying overnight and one of those, a guy from Scotland, started a conversation with me in the pub. We chatted away for a while before he began to turn the conversation onto dating and such and was actually beginning to chat me up when I stopped him and said, 'Before you waste your time, I do have a prior engagement for tonight, besides I swing towards women.'

He looked quite stunned, poor chap, but on that note, I finished my drink and went to the bus stop to meet my father; as his bus came into view I got butterflies in my stomach. There were quite a few people at the bus stop and I was hoping and praying my father wouldn't address me as 'Son' or 'Dave' the moment he stepped off the bus. I don't know why I worried about it. As my father stepped off the bus he looked me up and down and said, 'Wow, Lisa, you look stunning.' My butterflies instantly fluttered away. I never expected such a great compliment and I was beaming with pride as we set off to the first pub on the little 'pub crawl' I had planned for us.

Due to my father's bad hips, he couldn't stand up for long and so in each pub the aim was to find a seat. The first pub wasn't overly busy and we found a table quite easily and spent an hour or so chatting about things, mainly what was going on in the small world that was Tadcaster and about me telling everyone at work and how great they had been about it.

Soon we were in the another pub, this one was very busy though and the only spare seats were at a table with two other guys so we joined them and we all got chatting and generally had a good laugh with them. When our glasses were empty my father suggested stopping for another so I got up went to the bar, all of about five feet away from our table; whilst ordering the drinks I clearly heard one of the guys say to my father, 'Phwoar, mate, how did you pull a stunner like that?'

I instantly feared what my father was about to say but at the same time I was flushed with pride at how a stranger could think I was stunning; I mean it's almost a father's duty to compliment their off-spring but this guy had no reason to be complimentary.

'Do you mind, she is my daughter!' my father stated matter-of-factly.

Wow, that was a much bigger compliment than saying I looked stunning when he met me off the bus, he had got my gender right without even thinking, and he'd referred to me as his daughter.

I was up in the clouds, so happy with the acceptance shown by my own father in that statement. I had feared he could have said absolutely anything, possibly even reveal the fact I was not genetically female, even start a punch-up, but he calmed the whole situation.

The atmosphere at the table had changed with that and there was decidedly less banter between us all, it didn't take us long to polish off our drinks and head for another pub. The rest of the night was spent in a few pubs having fun chatting about all manner of things and all too soon it was time for the last bus home for my father, so I saw him onto his bus and went to another pub for a couple of drinks and to reflect on what had turned out to be a truly amazing night.

The next morning, I headed to Tadcaster to have yet another go at getting through to my mother and to tell my aunty and uncle about my plans to change gender. Until now, only my father and cousin knew. I would include my mother as knowing but it hadn't appeared to have registered with her; today I was going to make sure it did.

I stopped off first at my aunt's house and told them all about my plans. My aunty was really pleased for me and instantly noticed my painted red nails and wished me well for the future, then it was onwards to my mother's flat. For once, I had caught her in a sober moment and I could explain everything to her. I still felt unsure that she understood it all or even took it all in, so I wrote in her address/phone book my new name next to my old name and in brackets I put 'from August 2013'.

To finish off a busy weekend I was up north near Durham the following day visiting friends and finally to sign my deed poll and post-date it for 4th July. Sue, my closest friend and someone whose shoulder I had shed many tears on, was my choice to witness the deed poll. I was asked why I had picked 4th July. I chose it simply because it would be extremely easy to remember, being American Independence Day, and it would also signify my own new-found independence and the start of my new life as Lisa; I also joked I could be like the Queen and have two birthdays per year, my actual birthday and the birth of Lisa.

It was whilst we were up in Durham that I got a phone call from my aunty; she informed me that after I had left my mother's flat she had phoned round everyone in her phone book to tell them that I was changing my name to Lisa and growing breasts!

I brushed it off with something like, 'Well people will find out at some point,' although I did feel disappointed that my mother had outed me like that.

But then my aunty followed it with, 'Your brother has posted all over Facebook about it and the comments he's made are not very nice.'

'Oh, right, I don't have Facebook; do you know what he has posted?' I have never got on very well with my brother and we have avoided each other where possible for years.

It turned out that my aunty didn't have Facebook either but her granddaughter did, so I asked my aunty to pass on my mobile number and to ask Claire to text me what my so-called brother had posted on Facebook. Claire was very reluctant at first, she said I would not like what James had posted and she didn't want to hurt my feelings, but I persuaded her to tell me word for word.

Reluctantly Claire gave in and said, 'My brother Dave is having a sex change and growing some breasts, he's always been a cunt, now he'll have some tits to match.'

Claire added that lots of people had posted their own comments in response and they were all condemning my brother, but that didn't matter to me.

Yes, I was hurt by his comments and I was also bloody angry too, and at that moment I wanted to rip his head off, but the friends that I was staying with managed to calm me down, telling me that regardless of him being a relative he just wasn't worth my time or effort. I decided to ask Claire to post a reply on my behalf stating that from that day forward I no longer had a brother and that he was now officially disowned by me.

All my relatives, bar none, voiced their disgust at my now former brother and gave me their full support in my venture towards becoming a woman, which I found really uplifting.

A couple of weeks later I planned to go out round York for a few drinks. I knew that some of the girls from work were meeting for a birthday night out for one of the till staff, starting the night in the Nag's Head. So, I thought I would pop along early, say hello and then go my own way and leave them to it. Besides, it was time people started to see Lisa in the flesh.

I started on my own a bit earlier and had no problems, then the first of the girls arrived, we went into the beer garden where it was less noisy so we didn't have to shout to each other and had just about given up on any others arriving when finally, another four of my work colleagues arrived.

We had lots of great conversation, a lot if it about me and my progress and not once did anyone slip up and call me Dave. Another couple of drinks there, and the next thing I knew there were ten or twelve in our group, all from work and a couple of them not recognising me at first, which was another good sign: it meant I didn't stand out from the crowd, and I blended in quite well and looked every inch an ordinary female.

From the Nag's Head, we ventured down the road to 'Reflex' an 80s bar that was packed. Again, I had no issues despite a few in there being quite drunk. If I was going to encounter any bother, it would most likely come from people who were drunk. It was so packed in there that we lost some of our group, and we had no chance of being able to sit at a table in a group and it was so noisy that conversation was impossible, and for the first time I began to feel a little uncomfortable. I say uncomfortable because I had a coat with me; it was chilly once the sun had gone down, and not being able to sit meant hanging my coat over my handbag. It was never going to be put on the floor, which was wet and dirty, and it meant my bag was then quite heavy on my shoulder. I began to feel I had made a mistake taking my coat out with me in the first place.

Whilst there I heard a comment being passed around the pub, 'Tranny' or 'There's a tranny,' and I began to visibly wilt. I began thinking I couldn't survive the rest of my life with comments like that being thrown at me. Then suddenly someone tapped me on my shoulder and said, 'There's a tranny over there,' pointing to the corner of the pub. I breathed the world's largest-ever sigh of relief, but instantly thought about those horrendous attempted suicide figures and what I might have done had that comment really been aimed at me. Or if I had got comments like that when I first stepped out in public as Lisa. Whilst I felt relief, I also felt extremely sorry for the person who bore the brunt of those derogatory comments.

To this day, I have never seen the person the comment was aimed at that night. Was that person stepping out in public for the first time? Testing the waters to see if they could go through with transitioning?

Another of our group looked uncomfortable too, and I had mentioned earlier to her about a pub I normally call into where the music is more to my taste. She asked if we could go there, so I warned her the music might not be to her taste, nonetheless she said she'd feel better there than in Reflex, so we said our goodbyes to our group and went to the Artful Dodger.

In the Artful Dodger, I learned a lot about my workmate, and she learned a lot about me. Of all the people I saw daily at work, I thought she would be the one to 'reject' my news when first told. She didn't, but she didn't voice any opinion either. In our conversation, I found out that she enjoyed pretty much the same music as me, and used music to do tasks around the house or to lift her mood, and she used the same music that I do for the same chores/moods. I found out that she was far more liberal and open-minded than I had her down for, and whilst at work she is a bit of a miserable, moody little Hitler, away from work she is kind, warm-hearted and a lovely person all round.

She found out pretty much my life story, apart from my BDSM side, and was nearly in tears on hearing about my childhood bullying. She asked questions, and some were quite personal, but I answered every question. She told me she was unsure how to take my news at work, but on seeing me as Lisa, and hearing of my life story, she was now 100% supportive and even suggested that I write a book about my journey, which I laughed off at the time saying that nobody would be interested in the life of someone like me.

Time passed us by, and as the drinks flowed, so did the conversation and when we were finally kicked out due to closing time, we staggered together to the taxi rank and went our separate ways and I knew then that I had another good friend at work.

My taxi ride home was full of conversation too, all light-hearted banter, and when I reached home the taxi driver commented how lovely I looked and how pleasant our banter had been, and that he hoped to have the pleasure of being my taxi driver the next time I was out in town. Now that was indeed a lovely compliment and a lovely way to end a wonderful night out with the girls.

In my severely drunken state, the stairs at home 'attacked' me and made me fall up them; good job it wasn't down them! And then my housemate's bedroom door jumped out and slammed into me! Bad door! No damage done to me or the door, and so I stumbled into my own bedroom and flopped into bed. Happy, contented but quite drunk.

Sixteen

Independence Day

July and American Independence Day quickly arrived, I had posted off my signed deed poll a few weeks earlier and was now all set to commence the arduous task of changing my name with the banks, council, work and numerous other places. Wherever you have any form of account, club card, email, absolutely everything in your former name must be changed over to your new name.

I had been preparing for this day for some time now and I had written hard copies of letters ready for every name change I had to complete; all I had to do was edit the company and reference number and print it off. I had a hard copy for those who accepted a photocopy of the deed poll and one for those who required the original or legal copy.

When I ordered my deed poll I also ordered four legal copies as well and had already decided to send out four letters per week and worked out that it would take around eight weeks to get them all posted. Those who needed a legal copy of the

Me as Dave circa 1981 for the annual school photo.

Me circa 1990. I won many trophies playing pool, prior to my transition.

Me as Mrs. Santa and Sarah as Mr. Santa – Christmas 2013.

Me doing a radio interview at Minster FM talking about my transgender workshop.

Me with the amazing Stephanie Hirst at York LGBT Forum AGM, 2016.

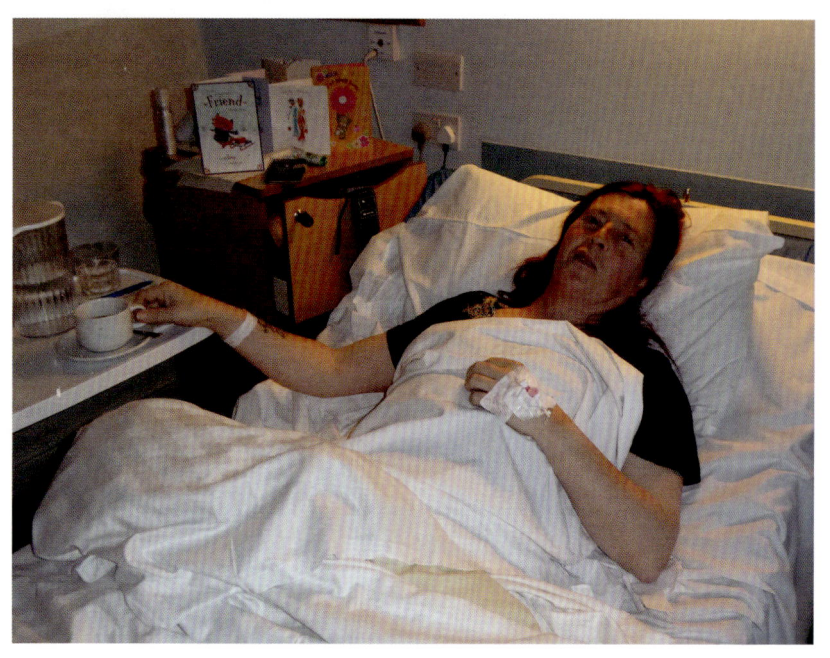

Me recovering in hospital after my gender realignment surgery, this is 3 days after the surgery, Dec 2016.

*Me with David Hoyle and Tanya Rabbe-Webber for
Portraits Untold at Beningbrough Hall, Gallery & Gardens.
Credit to Portraits Untold & National Portrait Gallery for the image.*

Me speaking out in public against the treatment of gay men in Chechnya, 2017.

deed poll were also sent a stamped addressed envelope, for the return of my deed poll.

Of course, there were a few that I could do in person just by taking the deed poll with me and on that day of freedom from my old life, July 4th, I went to my GP and got my name change process started with them first and of course work was also done the same day too.

With the smooth progress with everything at work and the fact that most of the staff had already seen me as Lisa, Helen suggested bringing forward my start date as Lisa to the Monday after my name had been changed on the system, probably the 15th or 22nd July, as I also needed my blouses ordering too. I was quite excited and ready in myself, so I said, 'Yes, why not, as soon as I have my blouses, I'll start as Lisa.'

On July 4th itself, before the store was open, Sarah used the tannoy to say, 'Good morning, Lisa.'

Another tannoy very quickly followed, 'Good morning. Can Dave come to admin, please.' It was the assistant manager, Chris, and the tone of his voice suggested he was not very happy. In the admin office, I was told in no uncertain terms that my name was Dave; I wasn't Lisa until later that month once my records had been changed and I must stop demanding people call me Lisa. Sarah was told exactly the same thing. I began to explain that Sarah knew the importance of that day to myself and that the store was closed, that it was just a 'congratulations' on my deed poll becoming legal and that I hadn't demanded anything. It made no difference to Chris and he left me feeling deflated on a day when I should have been riding high on cloud nine.

Within a few days, the letters started to come back to me confirming my name change, and on their return, more were posted out. On my day off that week, I called into the bank to change my name there. Obviously, as I was now living full-time as Lisa, except for at work, I went as Lisa.

The assistant who dealt with me was exceptionally nice and polite. She went through the whole process referring to me as Lisa all the way through and of course banks also need a specimen signature and just before I signed the form for that, she kindly reminded me to sign in my new name; it was a timely intervention as signing things in my former name was a habit that I had to get out of.

Everything went very smoothly with my change of name, that was apart from one company. This company had their head office in Dublin and so I wrote my letter addressed to their head office. When I got the reply from them the letter was addressed to my former title of 'Mr' and my former surname, the only thing they got correct was my first name. I was a little bit annoyed at this and I wrote to them enclosing another copy of my deed poll and explained that my actual new name was Miss Lisa Kelly and having the benefit of a colour printer I highlighted my name for them just to emphasise the point. A week or so later I got a new reply from them addressed to Miss Dave Kelly. You can only imagine my feelings at this point, it beggared belief that a company could cock up like that after having everything they needed twice and the essentials highlighted for them. Once I had calmed down I wrote to them once again expressing my disappointment at their incompetence and demanded that they process my change name correctly. They finally got my details right but it took them three attempts in total, you just couldn't make it up.

I would advise getting the name done first on your driving licence along with vehicle log book and motor insurance, but I was waiting for my latest batch of hormones to be delivered and that always meant collecting them the local sorting office as there was a small import duty and handling fee to pay, and any parcel collected from the sorting office required some photographic form of I.D. and not having a passport meant until they arrived

I could not send off my driving licence and with the parcel also being addressed to my former name I had to take along my deed poll as well; after all, I was not going to dress as a male just to collect a parcel.

Once I had my hormones, I sent off my driving licence and enclosed a legal copy of the deed poll together with a covering letter asking them to change the driver number code from that of male to that of a female. I had been advised that they would require a letter of headed note paper from my gender therapist, but I didn't bother with that, and as it turned out they changed my gender code without needing a therapist's letter. The gender code on the UK driving licence is the second number after the letters: males have a 0 or 1 and females have a 5 or a 6. For those born between January and September, the number will be 0 or 5 and from October to December your number will be 1 or 6, depending on your gender.

This stage of my life should have been a happy time for me; unfortunately it was anything but happy, it was a very stressful time and to compound matters I hit a financial headache. All the household bills were paid out of my account and my two housemates gave me their share, at least that's how it was meant to work, but over the previous few months one housemate was constantly paying me late and on occasions very late and the other housemate paid me short a few months in succession and the shortfall by now came to over a full month's worth of bills.

The bills always went out of my account at the start of each month and with their combined debts to me in July it sent me past my overdraft limit and I began picking up bank charges. With the household bills themselves going unpaid by the bank in July it meant that when they reattempted to collect payment it clashed with the rent payment; we all paid our rent and council tax individually. That left me without a penny for over two weeks and just enough food to get by for a week. Petrol for the motorbike to get to work was also an issue as a full tank would last me two weeks, but at that time I only had a quarter of a tank and the prospect of walking nearly seven miles home each day was looming large.

I was in a rut and depressed; it showed in my work too. I enjoyed my work and I took pride in doing it right and doing it well, and although I maintained a good standard through this latest depression I was not happy and not very chatty, and my workmates noticed.

I needed to place my next order of hormones around this time too and with no funds I was now facing the grim reality of being without hormones for a while. A gap in any medication is never good but with hormones it would play complete havoc with my body and mind.

Almost in desperation, brought on by struggling to get any money owed to me from my housemates, I tried to get a loan from a website but the major problem I faced there was that my name didn't match up. My name change was an on-going process and while it remained on-going I would not be able to get any credit at all, and the bank certainly wouldn't help. They were insisting I paid off my overdraft in full at the earliest opportunity and were about to commence reducing my limit by a set amount per month, so even though the bank knew me and could vouch for my new identity, they too use credit reference agencies to decide on approving loans and my name just didn't match where it needed to match. And then, on top of everything else, my bike broke down and I needed a part for it that would cost £100.

Even if I managed to get everything my housemates now owed me, it would not solve the problem, just ease it, as I was now fighting against bank charges that just kept me on the edge of my overdraft limit. As much as I tried, I could not see any solution and for the first time in my entire life I considered ending my life. I pondered how I could do it and indeed where I could do it, and each time I started to think about a certain method my mind got drawn to the people in my life and how they would be affected.

No matter how low I was at that time, I could not go through with ending my life. I didn't try, but the thought stayed with me for a few weeks, and I began to get an understanding as to how other people feel and the thoughts and fears they have as they contemplate or even attempt suicide.

What I needed was a lottery win. Not a jackpot – I wasn't greedy – but enough to allow me to breathe and regain control of my own finances. The main flaw in that plan, apart from needing an awful lot of good fortune, was the lack of money to even buy a lottery ticket. My lottery win came in the form of Sue. She asked how much I needed to get out of my current hole and promptly gave me a one-year interest-free loan and with a new hope, my mood lightened.

But just as my life looked like starting to improve, my curse of having bad luck descended upon me once again: I hurt my back at work and went off sick for two weeks. It wasn't an accident at work, I had just been kneeling on the floor filling the bottom shelf with stock, and when I tried to get up, I felt my back tweak and I couldn't move. Honestly, my life motto should really be: 'If it wasn't for bad luck I would have no luck at all.' I may even ask for that to be put on my headstone when I finally slip off the edge of the world.

I was prescribed some exercises to do for my back by the doctor and on the first day I attempted them I found myself stuck on the floor on my back with no one else at home. I remained stuck for over two hours before I managed to roll myself over and get up, and throughout my two weeks off work I got increasingly more and more bored and frustrated. I couldn't do very much to ease the boredom, I liked to go for walks, sometimes short walks, sometimes long walks, but I enjoyed being out in the fresh air and I couldn't even do that due to my back.

Then I read through my blogs on the BDSM website that I was a member of and when I reached the blog about the girls' night out I was reminded of what had been suggested to me, that I write a book about my life journey towards becoming a woman, and so I began to write. I spent most of my time off sick writing and rewriting and began to feel my depression lifting too. I felt as though I had a purpose in my life, that somehow at some time in the future my writing would help someone in some way. Once I had the first few chapters written I asked a couple of people to proofread them for me and to give an honest, critical assessment of my writing.

Overall, the response I got was amazing and gave me the encouragement I sought to continue. I did need to tweak little things here and there and put more information in at certain points, but I had something to work on.

Seventeen

Lisa starts work

Throughout my two weeks off sick, I kept the manager fully informed of my progress. She was a little bit off with me but then she was the same with anyone who was off sick. When I phoned to inform her that I would be back at work the following day, albeit on light duties, she was back to being quite chatty and cheerful.

'Are you coming as Lisa?' she asked.

'No, I have no uniform yet, but I will do once I have some uniform,' I replied. I hoped that what I had asked to be done, that everyone be informed that I would be Lisa on my return to work, had been done, I certainly didn't want anyone to be shocked when they saw me as Lisa; I continued with 'Has anyone raised any concerns or issues about me?'

'Not one issue,' she replied.

'Great, see you tomorrow then,' I said.

Next day I was at work doing light duties and hoping my blouses would arrive. It got past the usual courier delivery time and it looked like my blouses were not going to be delivered. A new order was placed and guaranteed next-day delivery asked for, and on the back of that, I said I would begin life at work as Lisa the next day. It would mean starting my shift in a shirt and changing into my blouse once it arrived, but I just thought I'd waited long enough and if the blouses were going to arrive mid shift I could cope with a few hours in a shirt.

I went home very excited about finally being myself at work from the following day. I had a spring in my step, albeit a careful step, my back was still aching so as much as I wanted to sing and dance with joy, the best I could muster was a badly out of tune song.

The following morning I was awoken by the sound of my alarm blasting out at 4.15am. Unusually, I had slept soundly but on waking I found myself consumed by nerves. I had just one hour to shower, dry and style my hair, apply my make-up, check my emails, get dressed, take my hormones and set off for work. I knew all eyes would be on me so my make-up had to be perfect. Normally, when I wasn't worried about what people might say or think, I could apply my make-up in around ten minutes.

Knowing I needed it to be perfect, and with my hands shaking, it took me almost three quarters of an hour; in the end I was rushing around to get myself ready to depart for work. It was almost like stepping out in public for the first time all over again, I was waiting for that first lingering look, or snigger, and I was on edge, far from my usual confident self. The whole of my shift I was nervous, I wasn't sure how each customer would react, the staff were great all saying positive things, but each customer was a different and unknown entity.

What I wanted to avoid was the strange looks, that lingering look that says, 'I'm not sure what to make of you.' I very much doubted any customer would cause a scene, but I did fear that knowing look, or overhearing a whispered derogatory comment.

I did have one customer ask me why I wore a shirt and not a blouse like the other ladies and I told her that my blouse had ripped and that I'd borrowed a shirt from the stores whilst a new blouse could be delivered. It seemed the easiest option, and it satisfied the customer. Other than that, the day went trouble-free. By the end of my shift I was bouncing around without a care in the world and indeed the next few days also went hassle-free, but it just wouldn't be me if there wasn't a 'but'.

That 'but' came on the Monday, which was stocktake day at work. With an hour and half left of my shift, I was called to the manager's office.

'Lisa, I have had a few complaints about you using the ladies' locker room and toilets, I want you to vacate the ladies' immediately and use the disabled toilet.'

'Hang on, the agreement was that if there were any unresolved issues at the time that I commenced as Lisa then I would use the disabled toilets for a short period whilst they got sorted out, not start as Lisa and then use the disabled toilet a few days later; they have all had a good two months to raise any issues,' I replied.

The news that a few had complained had not really surprised me; I was more shocked at not being asked if I minded using the disabled toilets from the next day whilst the manager dealt with the issue.

Helen responded with, 'Yes, I know, but rather than cause animosity you have to vacate the ladies' immediately.'

'You are aware that I have a legal right to use the ladies and being told to use facilities designated for less-able-bodied people is discriminating against me?' I was far from happy at this stage. Had I been asked rather than told, I most likely would have complied on condition it was sorted out swiftly.

'Well, I need to check that out with HR, I shall send an email straight away and get the ball rolling on dealing with the issue,' Helen remarked in a stern voice.

'Whatever,' I said, feeling badly let down by now, and with that I stood and left her office.

I went straight to the ladies' and began moving my stuff into the disabled toilet, it was extremely humiliating and degrading and I was raging with anger at not being allowed to finish my shift before vacating to the disabled facilities. Usually on stocktake days I stay way beyond my finish time but that day I was out of the building bang on the dot. I was close to tears and I just wanted to get home, away from work, and try to make sense of the bombshell that had knocked me for six. All I could think about was why on earth Helen had not made a phone call to HR for advice before speaking to me; at the very least HR would have told her how to go about things tactfully.

I had a much-interrupted night's sleep, my mind wouldn't settle at all and my confidence was shattered. The next day I fully expected a response from HR via Helen, but it never came. By this stage I was feeling down and resorted to just doing my job and going home on time, something that was unheard of from me; in the past I had always stayed a little over my time and quite often over an hour beyond my finish time but my confidence was shot and my own self-motivation was at a low ebb.

Wednesday came and went, and still nothing. It should have been one of the happiest times of my life, but I was down in the dumps and had zero motivation. Then on Thursday morning whilst Helen was doing her shop floor walk I noticed she had not closed the email screen so I sneaked a peak. I saw the email she had sent to HR on Monday: she had put that I had previously agreed to use the disabled facilities until after my final operation to become a full woman. I was extremely angry at seeing this as I had only agreed to use the disabled toilets if there were any unresolved issues at the time I commenced as Lisa, and I would certainly never have agreed to not using the ladies' until after my final operation.

The reply from HR was also there, dated Monday, and that did back me up by stating that I was being discriminated against if I was not permitted to use the ladies'. Worse followed though. I noticed Helen had replied to that email by saying she had sat down and had a meeting with me and that I had agreed to use the disabled toilets until Helen could inform the staff that I was entitled to use the ladies', and that she would do that on her return from two weeks' holiday which also coincided with me starting my two-week holiday.

That email was a pack of lies, Helen had hardly spoken a word to me since Monday let alone held a meeting with me. Now I was really fuming. The email back from HR said that if I had agreed to that, then it was fine to inform the staff whilst I was on holiday and then Anna, head of HR offered to spend a couple of days at our store during Helen's holiday to speak to any staff with any issues surrounding me and she gave a couple of dates too.

I now faced a dilemma: I knew Helen had basically told a pack of lies to HR but I couldn't confront her with what I knew. I really wanted to see Anna when she came to the store, but again I couldn't let on that I knew what had been written about me was false. Armed with what I knew, I could almost certainly get Helen suspended and most likely moved to another store, but I could not prove that no meeting took place and despite what I could claim, there was nothing in writing to back up what I had actually agreed to, so it would be word of mouth and my word against my manager's word, and I quickly concluded that I would most likely lose a grievance whilst stirring up a bucket load of trouble for myself.

Despite not being able to declare that I had seen the emails, I still printed them off and kept them safe; they could prove vital at some later date.

I had a bit more of a spring in my step for the remainder of my shift, fully expecting Helen to speak with me to confirm that HR agreed with what I had told her on the Monday, but Thursday passed with no word from Helen and I went home feeling frustrated. Why was she not telling me anything? The last of the emails were dated Wednesday so she had sat on the information for two days now. Friday was Helen's last day before having two weeks off. Surely she must speak to me before her holiday?

I was determined I was going to speak to Anna when she visited our store, I even worked out what I could say that could trigger her to question if I had indeed had a meeting with Helen after Monday's stocktake. It was pretty late on during my Friday shift when Helen finally spoke to me. She did it whilst we were outside having a cuppa and she skimmed over the subject using completely different information to what I had read in the emails.

I didn't say much in response, I was bitterly disappointed with how she had handled the whole issue and stunned that she chose to inform me what HR had said whilst we were outside and not in the office. I just said OK and added that I wanted all future meetings to be followed up in writing to avoid any possible future misunderstandings.

She could see that I had been down in the dumps all week and she had a great opportunity to lift my spirits and increase my own productivity but she failed miserably, and also finally proved to me that I could no longer trust her, I had lost all of my respect for her.

I was still less than two weeks into my work life as Lisa and what should have been a happy, almost euphoric time for me was the complete opposite. I was down and depressed. I had lots of people asking why I wasn't happy now that I was finally Lisa at work.

Aside from the issue over the facilities I could or could not use at work, I was still going through the process of changing my name and now that I had made the final HP payment on my bike, I wanted a car. All attempts at getting credit for a car had failed and although my finances were better than just a few weeks earlier, the apparent lack of any chance of getting a car was playing on my mind on top of the work issues and combined with everything else I just felt emotionally drained and mentally exhausted.

Work-wise, everyone was making the effort to get my name right, correcting themselves when they slipped up and apologising, which was fantastic. I really appreciated the effort everyone was making, that is everyone except for one person: so far, she had not made any attempt to address me as Lisa and made no apology either. I knew people would make mistakes, that was to be expected, after all, everyone had kept their name, it was my name that had changed and they were always going to find it hard after knowing me as Dave for so long. I knew that for a while this would be OK, but the fact that one person was making no attempt all was getting to me.

I sought advice, but not from Helen, I no longer had any trust or confidence in her, I sought advice via a confidential helpline. They informed me that before I could take any formal action, I needed to remind the person in question that my name was now Lisa and that I thought, in my opinion, that she had made no effort to address me as such, and that she had to start making the effort as it could be classed as bullying. They also recommended that I stress to her that I expected people to make mistakes for a while, but making the effort was the most important thing.

The very next time she called me Dave, I took her aside and followed the advice to the letter but by then it was her last day before starting her holiday and by the time she returned I would be on holiday, so I just had to hope that she remembered what I had said once we were both back at work together.

The date of Anna's first day at our store arrived, but it was my day off and as much as I wanted to see her, Chris had told me that she would be in a meeting for a couple of hours with the regional manager and unavailable and he couldn't give me a time to come in to see her as he didn't know what time the meeting would be, so reluctantly I agreed to wait until the second visit.

Afterwards I found out that nobody had gone to see Anna; I wasn't that surprised as all the people who I suspected had complained about me were either, like me, on a day off or were on holiday.

The day soon came for Anna's scheduled second visit and I was looking forward to my turn to speak to her. I had everything prepared in my head and was eager to see her, but as the day wore on it became clear that she wasn't coming. On asking Chris, he told me matter-of-factly that she had to go to another store today and would reschedule.

So, that was another thing I had to put on hold, but by now I was back to being quite cheerful and working my socks off. I had made up my mind to make sure neither Helen nor Chris could question my commitment or my productivity, not that they could before this episode. Maybe it was just me being a little on the paranoid side and thinking that they might decide that the whole issue surrounding me and changing gender was too much for them, too much in the way of paperwork and problem sorting and that they may attempt to drive me out by giving me unrealistic workloads, followed by disciplinary action on the grounds of not achieving my expected workload. Undoubtedly, I was probably being over-sensitive and paranoid, but if I got through my workload they wouldn't have that option.

By the time that I finished work on my final shift before my holiday I was shattered and ready for the break and I knew when I returned it would be September and the start of what we call silly season, the run-up to Christmas and the heaviest workloads of the year. From the middle of September right through to Christmas, the workload was always hectic, but just for once I was looking forward to it.

Eighteen

A return to Tadcaster

As confident as I was about going out and about around York, I began to think about my family in Tadcaster; how would I be able to visit them?

I was extremely nervous about even going to Tadcaster on the bike and walking a short distance to my father's house or my mother's flat, and that was despite wearing a big bike jacket and leather jeans, but I knew at some point in the future I would have to face people in Tadcaster because there would be family functions to attend.

The likelihood of bumping into any of my former tormentors weighed heavily on mind, and by now, due to my estranged brother posting on Facebook about me, I was quite certain that the news about me changing gender would have travelled all over town including to those who had taken delight in bullying me throughout my youth.

During my two weeks off work I had done a photo shoot and been out around Leeds but I was growing bored, I had nothing much to do and even less to occupy my mind, so I gave my father a call and without thinking just asked if he fancied a lunchtime drink in his local pub in Tadcaster. He jumped at the chance, it would save him the trouble of getting a bus to York to see me, and so we agreed on a couple of days later. As soon as I put the phone down I started to wonder why I had suggested a drink in Tadcaster and began to worry about what I would do if I saw any of those bullies.

This time I would be going by bus so that I could have a drink, and the more I pondered seeing the bullies, the more I started to think, *You know what, sod them*. I was getting brave in my thinking but I had to bite the bullet some time and it may as well be sooner rather than later.

I hadn't seen my Aunty Mary and Uncle George for a few years. They were always the ones who made me hate Christmas; every year I would have to put up with them either at our house or we would go to their house. No matter what the argument was, they were always correct, even when they were blatantly wrong, and it made me begin to despise them, less Aunty Mary, more Uncle George, but they came as a couple. My aunty wrote a letter to me when she saw my name change and address in my mother's phone book. That letter made me change my thinking about them and so I decided whilst in Tadcaster I would pop in and see them, so I planned to pop in after the lunchtime drinks with my father.

As usual, with something new to experience, I didn't sleep very well the night before my planned trip to Tadcaster. I woke up far too early and as soon as my eyes were open the butterflies began stirring in my stomach. I took my time getting ready and went for the bus a little earlier than planned. All the way on the bus I was trembling, I wasn't sure what I would do or say if I saw one of my tormentors. As much as the female side of me was confident, bitchy and maybe a little gobby at times, I could not be sure that I wouldn't crumble at any comment from one of my tormentors.

It felt like a journey into the unknown for me and as the bus pulled up at my stop I tentatively stepped off and headed for my father's local watering hole. As luck would have it, just as I approached the pub, my father came around the corner from the opposite direction. At least now I didn't have to worry about entering the pub on my own to find some of my bullies there and no sign of my father. Before we even entered the pub, my father commented how nice my new hairstyle looked, I had been to the hairdresser's and had a trim plus some red highlights put in, but just the fact that he even noticed was fantastic considering in all the years he was with my mother he never once commented on a new hairstyle.

Inside he told me that we were meeting my cousin later in the Britannia, the main watering hole of my bullies, but I no longer cared if they were there or not; today I was happy, with each passing minute I was growing in confidence. Part way through our first drink my Uncle George came in. He was his usual self, quite uninterested in conversation unless it was a debate of some kind; he said hello and that was it, but that was George through and through and I didn't really expect anything more.

After a couple of drinks hassle-free we left and went to a pub about halfway along the route to the Britannia. Inside I got a small shock: I should really have expected it, but my mother was sat in the big bay window on her own, drinking. This had always been her local pub; and as well as the fact that she quite simply refused to quit the booze, and I really shouldn't have been at all shocked to see her in there. I was rather dismayed and disappointed though; after all, she was throwing her life away for the sake of alcohol.

Apart from my mother, we were the only ones in there. Out of a sense of duty more than anything else we went over and sat with her. The first thing I did was take her to task about drinking herself to death, but it went in one ear and out of the other. Shortly afterwards my father went to the toilet and I said to my mother, 'You do know who I am, don't you?'

She gave me a blank look then replied, 'Probably his latest floozy,' meaning my father.

'Mother! It's me, Lisa. Used to be Dave!' I exclaimed with an angry tone of voice. She just continued to look completely indifferent and then went back to staring out of the window.

By now it was fast approaching the time that my father had told my cousin that we would be in the Britannia, so we finished our drinks and set off. I was slightly deflated due to my mother. I was upset with her and her love of alcohol, I wanted my mother back, not the washed-out shell of a person that she had become.

And so, onto the next pub where Nicola would finally meet Lisa, I was very apprehensive about this next pub as any one of my tormentors could have been inside. We entered, got drinks and sat facing the whole tap room, where I could clearly see a few of my bullies sat drinking and expanding their beer bellies. They all had a good look at the young woman who had just entered with an older man on her arm, and then they continued to drink and talk.

Nicola hadn't yet arrived, she had phoned my father to say she had been delayed and would be there shortly. One of the bullies came over and spoke, "Scuse me love, what do you think of my hair?' it was bright orange along the middle and shaven down to a grade one at the sides.

'It's OK, I suppose,' I replied, and he went back to his mates and declared, 'Well she thinks my hair's OK, you lot have got no taste.'

Shortly after, cousin Nicola arrived and we chatted a lot. She had known about Lisa for some time and was genuinely pleased to finally see for herself that Lisa didn't look out of place. Whilst we were all chatting and having fun, another of my tormentors came over and just sat down and joined in the conversation. Within a minute or so he had moved onto attempting to chat me up. I was more than just a little annoyed that he had gatecrashed our table and conversation, so when he attempted to chat me up I shot him down with, 'Look darling, I'm more man than you'll ever be and more woman than you can handle, so kindly fuck off back to your mates and leave us alone.'

You should have seen his face drop, he looked completely stunned and shell-shocked. I had said it loud enough for his mates to hear and he was laughed out of the pub in sheer shame and embarrassment. Nicola, along with my father, was extremely impressed. They'd heard me talk of Lisa being a bit of bitch but they'd not seen it until that moment. Dave would have just curled up in a corner and allowed them to steal away anyone he was with.

I was stunned that I had managed to confront one of my bullies and come out well on top. I was satisfied that I had finally laid one of my ghosts to rest, although there were still plenty of bullies I had not seen and some of them were far worse than the one I had just dealt with so effectively.

It was fantastic catching up with Nicola and spending time with my father. He heard about how good my home-made curry tasted and so I promised to invite him round sometime to sample it himself, and Nicola fancied a night out in York with Lisa so that was another day to look forward to once we could arrange a date, but all too soon it was time to leave the pub and head to my Aunty Mary's. I made a call to let Aunty Mary know I was on my way, and by the time I got there she had a pot of tea made, it was always a pot of tea with Aunty Mary, never a teabag in a cup. Uncle George was already home and in bed for an afternoon nap but he had told Aunty Mary that he'd seen me.

Aunty Mary asked me what had made me choose to change

my gender, so when I told her about the feelings I that I had since childhood and the fact that Tadcaster wasn't the safest of places to pursue something like that, she fully understood why I got out of town when I did. She was aware of my childhood bullying and she was only surprised it had taken me so long to start the process of changing my gender. She commented on how well I looked and that my hair was lovely and then we got to talking about things in general. She told me that the cousin I never knew that I had would be visiting the following spring. I had only found out two years previously that my aunty had given a child up for adoption in the 1960s and as yet I hadn't seen my cousin, but on telling me all this she got the photo album out and went through a host of photos. I was surprised to find that she had a lot of photographs of me from my youth and on looking we could both see how feminine I looked even back then.

Time whizzed past and without knowing it I had been there almost three hours. It was time to say goodbye and head back into the town centre to the bus station and get myself home. All the way home I had a massive smile on my face; a day which could quite easily have been a major disaster for me had been an overwhelming success. My former brother and my mother apart, my family were right behind me and proud of me, and for the first time in my life I could honestly also say that I was proud of my family.

It was a good job I now had the full support of my family because in the months ahead when I finally made it to the Leeds Gender Identity Clinic, one of the most important things the psychotherapists look at is the position of the family in terms of being able to be there for support in times of difficulty.

Nineteen

Trouble-free?

So, I had got through my first couple of months as Lisa, and from everything I had been told and had read, from here on things were supposed to get easier. Obviously, there would still be ups and downs, but I had reached September relatively trouble-free. I say relatively trouble-free because, although everything was going well in the real world, on the internet site where I had started to blog and keep a diary of my transition, trouble was brewing.

Back in July, towards the end of the month when I was at a very low point, I had started to receive abuse in the form of nasty mail on the BDSM site where I was blogging about my journey. It started off with just the odd abusive mail but over the next couple of months it became far more frequent and much more abusive, even bordering on threatening. I turned to various friends for help in dealing with it, but much to my own disappointment the only help I was offered was in the form of 'Ignore it'.

When you are a transgender person with hormones running wild, every little negative thing builds up and slowly erodes your self-confidence, so this was the last thing I needed to be told. Couple that with a few other people chipping in with their thoughts on who might be behind it all and suddenly I began getting a little paranoid, blaming people without evidence or proof just because someone else hinted that it might be him, or could be her.

Sue, my best friend, hated a girl called Dawn; in fact they were sworn enemies. I myself had previously got on well with Dawn, but with misguided loyalty I became what I despised most: I turned into a bully and turned against Dawn. I was vicious in my written attack on one of her blogs and as soon as I had done it I felt deeply ashamed of myself, but it was too late, what I had done could not be deleted. I knew that Dawn was not behind any of my abusive mail, and I knew I would have to make up for my misguided judgement, but I also knew I would have to leave it and wait for the dust to settle. The problem was, on a public site, my actions provoked a massive increase in the abuse I got, and some of it was extremely personal.

Soon after my shameful attack, I noticed a window of opportunity. Dawn had done a blog about building bridges, about how time had passed since the days when she was perceived as public enemy number one, and I commented on her blog. I posted that with the passage of time most things can be healed and sometimes all it takes is just a small olive branch to be offered, however there are some things that will never heal purely because one or the other doesn't want them to be healed. That comment would later open the door for me to make amends with Dawn, but it was seen by Sue, and I was then seen to be consorting with the enemy.

Late September and we had another Whitby weekend. It would be my first officially as Lisa, but it would also be my last too. Most of the group who went to Whitby were of the same mindset: they all saw Dawn as their sworn enemy, which made for an uncomfortable weekend away for me because I was now seen as a traitor. Honestly, you could not make it up, it was like being a child in the school playground, only now I was Lisa and Lisa did not back down to bullies, so I stood my ground with them and spent most of that weekend away arguing with the very people whom I had considered to be my closest friends.

That was the beginning of the end of every one of those friendships. I came home from Whitby feeling down and saddened by the fact that some people could not see the effect their ways were having on others. Within a day of returning from Whitby I had yet another increase in abusive mail and one of the mails was a death threat, and contained my house number in the line 'I know where you live.' This freaked me out somewhat. It could have been a lucky guess as to the house, but I kind of figured that it wasn't a guess, and for the first time on that BDSM site I went public about the abuse I was getting, and mentioned involving the police. I hadn't involved the police at that stage, but hoped my red herring would scare people into not sending any more abuse in my direction.

My public blog about it got loads of attention from all over the world and many of my friends publicly stating that they were 'there for me' and that they had 'been my friend for a long time and will be for a long time to come'. It all made me think I had maybe made a breakthrough and that some form of peace would now descend on my life. How wrong could I have been, for as I started to click on people's names to write thank yous on their walls, I found that as they were publicly posting their support for me, they were also removing me from their friends list at the same time.

Talk about being kicked while you're down, and as for hoping it would all go towards slowing down or even halting the abuse I was getting, well, it had the opposite effect and increased overnight. I reached the stage where I decided I had to leave the site, for the sake of my own sanity, confidence and morale, so with a heavy heart I posted a farewell in a group for the Yorkshire region. I mentioned the abuse had reached such a level that I felt I had no choice in the matter and that the next morning I would be deleting my account, with that I went to Tadcaster and spent the afternoon having drinks with my dad.

Next morning, I read through the responses on the farewell thread, and with a tear in my eye I then started to read through the 70+ mails I had been sent since writing my farewell. The clear majority were nice and sincere and saying they were sorry that I felt I had to leave, but even when it was clear that the bullies had beaten me, I still got six more nasty abusive mails from them, but I concentrated on the sincere mails, replied to them all with tears now streaming down my face, and I then hit the 'delete account' button.

I sat and cried, not because I had been beaten, not because I had ended the abuse by removing myself from their view, but because I had spent years building up my profile. I had photos from old phones from my early days within the BDSM scene showing exactly how I looked and how far I had come, and I had blog upon blog about my journey from being Dave to becoming Lisa. It was all gone, deleted in an instant like lighting a match and watching the flame flicker out as the light it creates gets weaker and finally leaves nothing but darkness.

But I was Lisa now and I didn't allow bullies to beat me. They may have won that battle but I was not going to leave for good; I had a new account waiting in the wings that I had kept under wraps and under the radar of the bullies and those who had unfriended me at a time when I needed them. I knew at some point the bullies would find my new profile, but I was not going to let them win a second battle. The next one would be the one where I ended the war and defeated my troublesome, pesky bullies.

Twenty

Stress?

Stress, what's that?

At work, summer gave way to autumn. I had been Lisa for a couple of months and things had settled down from those nervous first few days. By now we were in the thick of putting on the new Christmas ranges; the workload for the Christmas layouts was always hectic and never ran stress-free. Couple that with Chris who, throughout the summer, had been 'nit-picking' my work, and by autumn he was pulling me to pieces with his fault-finding missions.

On one occasion, I asked for the following day's workload, the paperwork that showed us the shelf heights and product codes, and he spent ten minutes convincing me that he'd given me the entire week's paperwork and that I must have lost it. He hadn't given me the full workload for the week, I knew he hadn't, but still he managed to convince me that he had.

That was followed a couple of weeks later when he asked why I had put my staff on different jobs to the ones that he'd listed for them in his workload notes that he'd left on my desk. I told him that there hadn't been any note left for me, so I had put my staff on the jobs that I thought were the most important. Yet again, he tried to convince me that I must have lost his note, either that or I had disregarded his instructions, only this time I stood my ground. There had been no note left and I protested vigorously. A heated argument followed and over the summer I had learnt that he was 'never wrong' and that even when he was wrong he would not admit it, so with the words being exchanged getting ever closer towards attacking each other's personality, I held up my hand and stated matter-of-factly, 'That's it, end of discussion it's way past my finish time so I'm off,' and with that I stormed out of the office and went home in a horrendously foul mood.

On the Monday of the following week I had my annual review and in it he tore me to pieces, giving losing paperwork and his other nit-picking as evidence, and also stating that I was in a bad mood and grumpy more than I was 'normal or happy' and it was reflecting on my team and the customers, and then finished by stating I could not use my transition or being hormonal as an excuse and that I must show immediate improvement in all areas if I did not want to be taken down the disciplinary route.

I was fuming! How dare he? I was not happy at all and told him that it was all his stupid nit-picking that was making me feel that work was becoming more akin to serving a jail sentence and as for hormones, he should try it and see how he copes with forcing a 'second puberty' on top of a body that still generates male hormones whilst taking female hormones.

One of the things I had found out was that whilst I took testosterone blockers, the body still produced testosterone and taking oestrogen meant that whilst I was effectively going through a second puberty, there was also a war going on inside my body between the male and female hormones; think in terms of a teenage girl hitting puberty, and then a teenage boy hitting puberty, and put them both together and you get an atom bomb just waiting to blow.

So, back to autumn and the Christmas rush, with me feeling like work was a chore and in no mood to break into a sweat to get things done. My confidence had been sinking by the day, my mojo had got fed up and gone on holiday, I was getting grief at work from Chris and I was coming home to find I had no social networks that I was having fun on and very few actual friends who I could meet and pass the time of day. Once again, I sank into depression; it felt like I was still a million miles away from reaching the gender clinic and for the first time I questioned what I was doing in changing my gender, why was I so down despite living my life as Lisa? After all, it's what I had been aiming for all this time.

I had a spell where I went through the repercussions of what might happen if I suddenly stopped and changed back to being Dave. It was those very thoughts that made me also question why I was even alive; on several occasions I had questioned my role in life and if the world would be a better place without me being part of it. I had never acted on these feelings but I had come close a few times and in the run-up to Christmas, thinking I would probably find myself lonely and alone on Christmas Day, this was another of those times where I came close to planning the end of my life.

The problems I had at work because of Chris were steadily eroding my self-confidence. My self-esteem was taking a dive too with my ongoing internal hormonal fight making my moods swing almost daily I was finding it hard to cope with the thought of waking up each day and going to work.

I needed these mood swings to settle down and I needed something outside of work to occupy my mind. Whilst at York

Pride during the summer I had visited a stall, York LGBT Forum, and found they were looking for new volunteers and transgender people. It sounded just the thing that I needed, and so I joined, and at the AGM in November 2013 I was elected as transgender coordinator and joint events coordinator. Looking back, it was probably getting involved with York LGBT Forum and taking on those roles that saved my life. Without getting my teeth into doing something positive like helping other transgender people, it is highly likely that I would have attempted suicide. York LGBT Forum had given me a reason to live.

Back in July, Sue had lent me £300. At the time she had told me there was no rush to pay it back and that it was interest-free for a year. Knowing I had an accident claim to look forward to, we had agreed I would pay the money back when I received my insurance payout.

By November, though, given that we had now fallen out, she was chasing me to pay back the £300. I kept her informed on the insurance progress and kept her at bay, but by mid-December she was getting impatient as I had informed her that I had agreed a settlement in November and as advised by the insurance company, I should have my cheque by the start of December. It never materialised and after chasing them up I finally got the cheque two days before Christmas. Needless to say, it was a huge relief to get Sue off my back once the cheque had cleared.

With what I had left, around £3000, I decided to get myself a car. I hadn't even taken any lessons yet, but there were a few cars that I could legally drive on my motorbike licence and so I found one some 140 miles away in Peterborough and at the start of the new year I collected a microcar and was finally free of a motorbike helmet messing my hair up, which by now was nearly shoulder length and dyed dark red.

I began 2014 filled with new hope: I now had a car, I had some money left over and I had my first appointment at the gender clinic to look forward to once we reached the new tax year. My hopes took a blow within the first week of January though; my new car shed an engine mounting bolt and cost me £400 to repair, a few other minor problems, each one costing money, led me to decide on taking driving lessons.

As April arrived I was checking the post daily, anxiously awaiting a letter from the gender clinic at Leeds. In no time we reached the final week of April and still no sign of an appointment at the gender clinic. Out of desperation, I phoned them to ask about an appointment and was told the letter had been posted that very day. My appointment was at the end of May, a few days after the booking for my first driving lesson.

From cloud nine I was quickly brought crashing back down to earth with a bang at the start of May. We were given notice to quit the house as the owners had had their overseas contract terminated and wanted their home empty, to move back into themselves. We had to vacate the house by mid-July, so once again I found myself looking for somewhere to live.

Twenty One

The gender clinic

By the time of my first appointment at the gender clinic, I had managed to secure a room to rent and was busy getting the paperwork and bond arrangements sorted out in readiness to move on 1st July. I'd rearranged my rota at work to give me the day off for my appointment, and duly set off in my car, a bundle of nerves.

This first appointment was the most important day of my life to date, and each subsequent appointment would surpass that, but this was my first taste of the gender clinic. I parked with ease despite the very limited parking spaces. I was nearly an hour early such were my nerves, I just couldn't sit around at home waiting for the time to depart to arrive; besides, I couldn't afford to be late and gave myself plenty of time should I break down en route. I sat in the waiting room with a coffee from the vending machine and a packet of Mini Cheddars, watching as people came and went and the minutes passed towards my appointment time.

The form I had been given to fill in had been completed, the coffee long since finished, and then the minute hand on the clock showed it was time. The nervous tension building in the pit of my stomach was growing and I now desperately needed the loo but dared not leave the waiting room until someone came for me, so I sat there, crossing and uncrossing my legs. Finally, nearly ten minutes past my appointed time, Linda arrived and called out my name. I quickly jumped up and asked if I had time to dash to the loo before we got started, and with that I could get some relief.

Linda was lovely, she had a stunning figure and a personality to match and she quickly put me at ease while going through what happens, the options, the procedures, how the NHS system works and other things, and then we moved on to questions about me. This was almost a repeat of what I had gone through with the psychotherapist sessions over a year earlier, and there were to be two more appointments along similar lines that I had to get through before Linda would decide to enter me onto the gender care pathway, or not.

I sailed through that first session and was given a date for the next one for the end of June, and I returned home with my nerves settled and feeling full of vigour, excited about the journey ahead of me and ready to face the world once again. Just getting that first appointment behind me gave me a massive boost and that endless tunnel now appeared to have a small glimmering light at the end of it. Though it was still very distant, I could finally see it glowing in the distance.

I had a spring in my step at work and not even Chris could drag down my confidence, my facial hair removal was going well, and I by now I was getting through each day, no each week, without people giving me any strange or lingering looks. The only blight on my life was the ongoing harassment I was still getting from someone through the internet.

When I arrived for my second appointment at the gender clinic, Linda had a letter with her that they had received through the post anonymously. It claimed I was a dangerous predator who wasn't transgender but a psychopathic liar only changing gender for fetish and sexual reasons, and had pictures edited on Photoshop of me in compromising positions. These pictures were from a photo shoot I had done and the original photos were tasteful, although included elements of BDSM, but the pictures I was shown by Linda had been altered and showed me as prostituting myself.

The first ten minutes of that second appointment were spent explaining the harassment I was getting and that there was an ongoing police investigation about it, and I was given the letter to pass onto the officer dealing with my case. It was now clear that the person harassing me was out to ruin my life and I wondered what their next action would be.

Although that second appointment then went without a hitch, I left feeling numb and worrying about the person targeting me, the person I now called 'Eugene', as that was the name they had used on their letter to the gender clinic. Eugene had already emailed York LGBT Forum some months previously, to 'warn them' about me, and had copied in some national newspapers, so I now found myself under stress as to what Eugene's next move would be.

A couple of days later I got the keys to my new home, a multiple house share where each tenant had their own room but the facilities were communal, and I began moving my belongings into my room. I was loading my little car full to bursting on a night, going to work the next morning and stopping off at my new house on the way home to unload.

By July 4th I had moved in, but it had taken a toll on my little car and it once again shed an engine mounting bolt, another repair bill of £400, and I immediately decided I needed to step up my efforts to pass my driving test. My driving instructor told me I was ready, but I needed to send my licence off to change my address and then book the theory test.

Also by this time I had made peace with my brother James. We had had a good chat via Facebook and solved all our differences. Part of the reason I had always been at war with my own brother was because during our childhood he appeared to have his life mapped out whereas I was constantly battling my inner turmoil of not knowing why I felt like a girl but appeared to be a boy, so in a way I was insanely jealous of him.

August arrived and I had my all-important third appointment with Linda at the gender clinic, which went without a hitch and I was accepted onto the gender care pathway. That meant I was now on my way to being prescribed hormones and edging closer to the surgery I so desperately needed. Through those three sessions I had satisfied a few NHS hurdles in that I had provided proof of my legal name change via deed poll and supplied bank statements and wage slips dating back to my name change, which meant I had already completed the social aspect of 'living the role for at least twelve months' and I could move straight towards the next step of an appointment with the endocrinologist who could start the prescribing of hormones, but I would have to wait for an appointment.

Late August arrived and I took my driving theory test. This was the one aspect of passing my driving test that I feared. I was supremely confident of being able to pass the driving part of the test, but the theory part was giving me nightmares: it was the hazard perception side that worried me. In the theory test, I correctly answered every question but only just scraped through the hazard perception with the absolute minimum score needed, so overall on paper I had a comfortable pass and could now book my practical driving test.

I got the date of my driving test sorted out, Saturday 20th September, and I got my little car valued ready to do a part-exchange deal for a decent second-hand car that would see me through two or three years, and I began searching car dealers' websites looking at possible cars within my price range of £1000 part-exchange plus around £500 cash and looked at the possibility of finance of an extra £1000 for the right car. Things were looking up and going my way at long last. The only downside was my savings: with the car purchase and then the repairs to the car, along with moving house, my accident insurance payout had vanished.

The final Thursday of August saw me travel to Doncaster to see my BDSM friends. It was great catching up with them and the evening went well until around midnight when I gave one friend a lift home. Once I had dropped him off and got back onto the road home, I managed only five miles before a familiar sound caught my attention: the engine had shed an engine mounting bolt again!

I now had to nurse the car home, some forty miles away at night. All was fine for the next few miles, but then another mounting bolt parted company with the car and I was reduced to limping the car along at around 20mph. Still, it wasn't a complete disaster, I could get the car repaired, part-exchange it and top up the new car with a finance deal. Trundling along the A19 I got past Selby, a town about fifteen miles from home, and with each mile I was getting ever closer to making it home. The new plan was for my passenger to grab a taxi from my house to get to his house as with my car in the state it was in, I needed to get it home without taking any detours.

Somehow, I managed to limp my stricken car to within three miles of home when a third bolt parted company and with that the car came to a very noisy shuddering halt. It was now nearly 2am and I found myself having to join the RAC to be rescued and get my car home, after paying a joining fee and recovery fee, which took up any car repair money I had left. I finally got home just before 4am.

Suddenly my £1000 part-exchange had turned into about £150 scrap value and any hope of finance going for a burton too as I had only planned on a small amount of finance to top up what I already had to make sure the car I got was good enough to see me through a few years' trouble-free. To make things worse I now had no transport to get to work; my start time was way before any buses started and I certainly couldn't afford a taxi each day, so I had to go out and buy a cheap bicycle.

On top of everything else I needed to ensure I had a car again before the start of October, as I had my next appointment at the gender clinic, so the pressure for me to pass my driving test was now mounting; fail, and all my plans were sunk with no plan B to fall back on.

Twenty Two

Free to be me

During the year, I had been part of a team working on a staff LGBT awareness training course for the staff of care homes. It was a project organised by the York LGBT Forum and we hoped it would enable care home staff to have a greater understanding of issues LGBT people face when they go into care. We had named the project 'Free to be me' and spent the whole year rehearsing and re-scripting the whole presentation, but as we headed towards autumn we appeared no closer to being ready to pilot the presentation.

With the date of my driving test fast approaching, I searched high and low for a very cheap car that I could get a couple of years out of whilst I rebuilt my funds. Finally, I found one within my meagre budget of up to £400 and I travelled to Halifax by train to collect it without first seeing the car or test driving it, and I drove it problem-free back home just a couple of days before my driving test, which heaped more pressure onto myself to pass the driving test or have a car standing idle on the drive.

The day of the driving test arrived and I had a one-hour lesson prior to my test just to brush up on certain things. My instructor had been brilliant, and when given the choice of having him in the back seat for the test or waiting at the test centre, I opted not to have another pair of eyes on me during the test. I started the test badly by messing up the reversing into a parking bay, something I had always managed with consummate ease, and then on exiting the test centre I failed to check all my mirrors properly once I had made the turn onto the main road. These silly mistakes were quickly followed by a couple more basic errors and within a couple of minutes of starting my driving test I knew I had already amassed four minor errors and heading for a fail if I didn't improve.

I said to my examiner that now that I had got my silly errors out of the way, I was going to be faultless for the remainder of the drive, a bold claim under the circumstances, but I enjoyed the remainder of my driving test and genuinely thought that I had done well enough to pass.

On parking back at the test centre I was asked if I wanted my driving instructor present for the result, to which I replied with a yes. Once my instructor was in the back seat, the examiner said, 'When you told me you were going to be faultless for the rest of the test, you already had four minor faults, the rest of the test you were perfect, so I am pleased to inform you that you've passed with just four minor faults.'

I was jubilant! I was now officially a legal car driver. I really couldn't thank my driving instructor enough, he had been amazing throughout my lessons and we had a good laugh too, but now I had to calm down again because that evening I had the first of my new events. I had started a monthly transgender-specific social night out, a place where anyone under the transgender umbrella could have a night out in York instead of having to travel to Leeds or Manchester, so now for me, it was a double celebration. The night was a huge success, extremely well attended and it made me think about what else I could do for other transgender people.

I soon found myself charging headlong into the Christmas rush at work, and my gender clinic appointment had gone very well. I had met the endocrinologist the same day as my standard appointment and had got my first hormone prescription via the NHS which meant I was instantly about £100 per month better off with no longer having to import hormones.

As ever though, there was trouble on the horizon: Eugene, my online harasser, hadn't gone away and was now emailing random people using disposable email addresses and TOR servers to mask their IP address. The random recipients of Eugene's emails included the City of York council and my head office at work. My Facebook profile at the time gave away where I worked, but I had no idea how Eugene had got details of the Council being interested in our 'Free to be me' project.

We had just had our AGM for the York LGBT Forum, and there had been a heated discussion over funding, with the solution coming from me, but it had caused a rift to open, which was documented via the minutes, and as minutes are distributed to the members and associate members via email, it occurred to me that maybe Eugene was on the Forum's mailing list. It was the only way that I could see how Eugene would know about our link to the council. The newly elected co-chair of the forum was also starting to try and impose 'martial law' on the subgroups; he wanted the forum to be a business and wanted the subgroups to have anything they wanted to do approved by the co-chairs, and he was particularly against the older persons' LGBT subgroup which was behind the 'Free to be me' project.

With January fast approaching, the co-chair tried to halt all rehearsals of 'Free to be me', which would have curtailed the planned pilot showings in early February to two different audiences. The other co-chair was part of the 'Free to be me' team, and in solidarity with her male co-chair, pulled out of the team. Suddenly, the whole presentation slotted into place and ran smoothly during a rehearsal, but tension within the Forum continued to rise and came to a head at the monthly open meeting in January. The discussions got quite heated surrounding 'Free to be me' and how it was going to be marketed. The main talking point was an outside company getting a sixth of any money made from it, but what couldn't be grasped was the outside company was responsible for and held the rights to one sixth of the content. During the meeting the secretary resigned.

A few days after that meeting, an extraordinary meeting was called by a few people, including both chairs and the treasurer. At the extraordinary meeting, the arguments continued and nothing was resolved; the male co-chair resigned and stormed out and left the female co-chair to finish and close the meeting, resigning the following day via an email she distributed to everyone without using the 'blind copy' option, thus revealing the email address of everyone on the mailing list.

After some hassle on Facebook, it suddenly became apparent that Eugene was indeed on the mailing list: Eugene's profile name on Facebook matched the name of one person on the mailing list and a new campaign against me via email came from Eugene.

Things looked very bleak for the forum, but we still had sufficient committee members to elect an acting chair and secretary, so a new extraordinary meeting was called, of which I would chair in an acting capacity. The purpose was to elect new officials and set out how the forum would be run. With the previous resignations, it was taken that we could run smoothly, but finding people to take over the vacated positions was hard.

I found myself as the female co-chair, a position I didn't really want, but I also didn't want to see the forum close, and with my male co-chair Jeff and acting secretary Jean we set about addressing the forum's money troubles. The previous female co-chair had bought merchandise for around £700 without forum approval and was now demanding that money back, which in effect would leave the forum with no funds, and she still had that merchandise in her possession. It was too late for us to buy more merchandise to sell, apart from not having the funds to do so.

Over the next few weeks the situation was resolved via a third party acting as a go-between, and we also received a £1000 donation. We had gone from almost bankrupt to being solvent in no time at all, and we also applied for charity status. On the back of our new-found charity status, we applied for funding for 'Free to be me' and won another £1000.

We had gone from turbulent January to steady May, and through that time my work life was very settled. Chris had moved to another store and Helen had gone too. Our new manager, Ben, was a steadying force for me, and I found him to be much more trustworthy and relaxed. Carol had been promoted to assistant manager and moved to another store, and Angie was our new assistant manager.

My gender clinic appointments were scheduled about every three months and were just standard until July, when I had a 'pre-first opinion' appointment. To be referred for surgery, you had to have what was called a first opinion and a second opinion, and this pre-first opinion appointment would give me a much better idea of what to expect for these all-important opinions. As it turned out, I was already pretty clued up due to the research I had previously done. I needed to show that I knew and understood all the possible risks and knew what they meant, and demonstrate why the surgery outweighed the risks involved whilst at the same time showing that I was level-headed and not pursuing a fantasy. I found the fantasy part quite disturbing in that all the previous psychotherapy sessions at local level and repeated at the gender clinic, together with each subsequent appointment, were partly designed to 'weed out' the odd fantasist, but I sailed through that session and looked forward to the actual 'first opinion' in August.

When August duly arrived, the 'Free to be me' project had been piloted, touched up, piloted again and had been delivered to our first few care home bookings, bringing in more funds for the Forum, and we had also started to develop the care home project into a workplace version, which we were now almost ready to pilot. In the care home version, I was getting rave reviews for my transgender awareness part and that was in turn building up my own confidence to speak openly in public about being transgender and raising awareness of the issues transgender people faced every day.

It was the start of a path towards speaking to larger audiences and public speaking, but from August onwards my focus was on my own journey and the build-up towards the forum's first AGM as a charity.

Twenty Three

First opinions count

The day of my appointment for a 'first opinion' soon arrived and I was very nervous about it; it was, at that point in my life, the most important day so far. I worried that I would not remember all the risks and possible side effects of the surgery that I so desperately needed. That first opinion would be with my 'lead professional' Linda, and the consultant doctor who had diagnosed gender dysphoria at my third appointment, the one which led to me being accepted onto the gender clinic care pathway, so they were not strangers.

With butterflies in my stomach I scraped through the first few minutes of the appointment before my nerves settled and I sailed through the remainder without a hitch and got confirmation of being able to move towards the 'second opinion'. The only downside from that first opinion appointment was being informed that Eugene had yet again sent a letter to the gender clinic, and followed it up with an email, yet another disposable email, and untraceable as far as the police were concerned.

The gender clinic was aware of my ongoing harassment and that the police were involved, but it played on my mind as to exactly how far would Eugene go. It was plainly obvious that Eugene was trying to get me thrown out of the gender clinic and ruin my life.

I already knew from previous appointments that I would have to travel to the gender clinic at Sheffield for my second opinion. However, the Leeds gender clinic could not even ask for an appointment until I had completed twelve months on prescribed hormones, which would be late November, and then I would be placed on Sheffield's waiting list which was running at eight months, making it late July the following year at the earliest. My other option was to pay privately for the second opinion, around £120, and travel to someone in Hull, but again I couldn't do that until the twelve months of NHS hormones had been completed, but at least with going private I would get my second opinion by late January or early February.

Life with York LGBT Forum was quite hectic, with two meetings per month, guest speakers to accommodate, both 'Free to be me' projects along with running my monthly transgender social night out and building up towards celebrating our charity status at the AGM. We were now on a stable footing again and gaining much more recognition than ever before which was leading to requests coming in to us for information and help.

One such request was for someone to give a talk about diversity and equality and to help with transgender awareness. It would be at Beninbrough Hall, a National Trust property, and they wanted someone to talk during February, so I was all set for my public speaking debut.

At the start of November, I got a letter from the gender clinic; they had now taken on another consultant doctor, which meant they could do second opinions 'in house' and they had a spare appointment towards the end of the month which they offered to me. Naturally, I jumped at it. It meant everything was fast-forwarded and I had little time to prepare myself mentally, but it would be taking a few months off my journey towards surgery and saving me from having to go private for a second opinion.

Just before my second opinion, I had my manager inform me that Eugene had sent yet more stuff to head office, and I found out that Eugene was also posting details of my workplace across social media and asking people to contact my work or head office to complain about me and demand that they take action against me. Head office were now investigating my social media content and my manager advised me to remove any link to my workplace from my social media profiles.

Fortunately, I did not have my workplace linked anyway, and head office took no further action, but as you can imagine, my head space was shot to pieces and my confidence ebbed away right when I needed to be sound and confident.

I then got the news from the garage, where my car was having its MOT, that I was looking at a big bill to cover the work that needed doing to get the car through its MOT, and I was starting to get that familiar sinking feeling again.

Had I cancelled my second opinion appointment, I could have faced a long wait for a new appointment, so I went ahead with it despite feeling down and lacking somewhat in confidence. The appointment was with someone I had never met and despite feeling even more nervous than I was for my first opinion, I sailed through completely untroubled by my nerves or the turbulence in my private life. I was pleased to be referred to my choice of surgeon, Mr Church, and to be referred to a further specialist for hair removal from the surgical area. Given that the hair removal from my face was still ongoing, and brought tears to my eyes, I was not looking forward to the genital hair removal at all.

I was told by Linda that my surgeon had a three-month waiting list and the referral letter would be sent at the start of December, so I figured with the Christmas and New Year break I would probably see my surgeon in February and possibly get my surgery by mid-summer. I also remembered that I had an account with South Yorkshire credit union and that my initial loan to help cover the bond on my new house had long since been paid off. I applied for and got £500 so that I could trade in my car for a slightly better one, one I hoped would last me a few years; I was on cloud nine.

Via a few friends, I found out where Eugene was posting on social media sites, and armed with a conversation we had previously had on Facebook when Eugene was unaware that I knew who they were, I decided once and for all to blow Eugene out of the water by posting our conversation complete with details of a so-called trap that Eugene had set for me. It was a simple link that Eugene had posted in our conversation and asked me for a response to the allegations about me; that link led to what looked like a broken web page, but it registered your IP address and Eugene had used this as 'proof' that I was trying to access other people's information.

The plan worked a treat; within hours of me posting my evidence to shatter Eugene's claims about me, Eugene deleted their profile from each social media site. I had finally got rid of my harasser and done it in style too.

At the Forum's AGM, we had managed to get the new MP for York Central to be our guest speaker, and we had the Lord Mayor of York to officially open the meeting too. Being our first AGM since becoming a charity we had certain regulations to follow which meant every committee member standing down. They could stand for election again, but it meant the election of our officials was more long-winded than usual, but the evening was a huge success and I was re-elected as female co-chair as well as the transgender subgroup coordinator. I stood down from the events post, though, as it would have given me too much to do.

Twenty Four

New Year, new hope

Early January came and to lift the gloom of a dreary month, I got my appointment through to see my surgeon, it was for April, and I also got my referral through for hair removal and set up a patch test for February. With that, I began working on the talk I was going to give to the staff and volunteers at Beninbrough Hall in early February. That would be followed a few days later with me giving a talk for LGBT History Month in York and another talk up in Newcastle also for LGBT History Month.

Bookings for 'Free to be me' were still coming in at regular intervals too, keeping me very busy, but I was all set to get even busier: I had been asked to do a live podcast for HLGBT Performing Arts, and that meant going live on the local radio to promote it. It was to talk about transgender issues and where I felt the transgender community would be in the future, and I gave a very good radio interview for Minster FM. I took to it like a duck to water and showed no sign of any nerves; I was cool, calm and composed throughout the radio interview.

A few days after that radio interview, I was in touch with Stephanie Hirst, who had heard my interview and had been quite impressed – high praise indeed coming from someone who had worked in radio for most of their life, and someone who was considered quite a celebrity, especially within the transgender community. Through our conversations, after mentioning the work I did with York LGBT Forum, she agreed to be our keynote speaker at the November AGM.

On the day of my talk for Beninbrough Hall, I wasn't the slightest bit nervous and began my talk with the subject of stereotypes and role models, before moving onto transgender issues and covering the lesbian and gay community too. The talk was exceptionally well received and I stayed behind afterwards to chat one-to-one with people.

One lady told me that my talk had done more for her than years of therapy; it turned out that her ex-husband had left her to be with another man, and the way I had explained how LGBT people often hide their true self away and feel compelled to hide behind a marriage and follow society's expected route whilst they come to terms with who they really are, had helped her to understand things a lot more than she had previously been able to.

My talk a few days later was vastly different; it was all about my own life from the early 1970s through to present day, and again it was extremely well received with a very good audience and lots of great comments afterwards. To say I was beaming with pride would be an understatement.

I had my patch test of hair removal a few days later, just before I was due to head to Newcastle for my next talk, and sandwiched between the two was my latest facial hair removal session. The patch test for genital hair removal was quite a nervy affair, I was naked from the waist down in front of a very good-looking young lady and I was scared that I may suffer the embarrassment of getting an erection, something I had not had to worry about for quite some time. I didn't need to worry though, it passed without an issue and strangely enough did not hurt half as much as the facial hair removal did.

My talk in Newcastle went even better than it had done in York and it was to a packed-out room with people having to stand due to the room being so full. I guess I was now a fully fledged public speaker and by now I had a couple more talks lined up.

February gave way to March and I had my first actual genital hair removal session, electrolysis, which was basically sliding a fine needle down the shaft of the hair and essentially frying the hair follicle with a blast of electricity.

The patch test hadn't hurt but this was more intense and left a warm feeling which grew ever warmer throughout the session. I was told by the young lady doing the hair removal that if needed, I could be ready for surgery by late June; my hopes of surgery sometime in the summer were growing.

Mid-March arrived and it was time for my live podcast. I had expressed concerns that the event was overpriced considering I was no celebrity and it was midweek in the basement of a pub, and my fears were confirmed when only two people turned up to watch live and potentially ask questions in the 'Q&A' section. Still, it was a live pay-per-view podcast, so there may have been a bigger online audience, and it would be available afterwards for people to download too. The podcast went extremely well from my point of view in that I answered each question put to me by my interviewer concisely and clearly and got across my point quite easily. The question and answer session at the end went well too, including some personal questions, which I always welcomed if only to give a better understanding of what being transgender meant.

I was completely unsure what to expect from my meeting with Mr Church; it was one area about which my extensive research had come up blank, so I decided to go after swotting up again on the risks and side effects of the surgery. There were a few different types of surgery available and I had opted for what was called a full vaginoplasty, basically a procedure which would use the skin of the penis to create a vagina, with the scrotum being used to create the labia minora and majora. The head of the penis would also be used to create a clitoris, so I would have a fully functioning vagina if all went well.

The morning of my appointment with my surgeon arrived after a sleepless night; I had too much on my mind for what I considered the most important day of my life. I really was a bag of nerves this time, visibly shaking as I got into the car for the forty-minute drive to the hospital. I pulled into a lay-by about five minutes away from the hospital and settled my nerves with a cigarette and then sprayed body spray all over to mask the smoke and nicotine smell, before I drove on to park at the hospital. I was still a good half an hour early and made use of the free drinks machine to get a hot drink in the waiting room. The wait did nothing to ease my butterflies and I nearly jumped out of my skin when my name was called a good ten minutes before my scheduled appointment time.

Almost instantly, Mr Church put me at ease and discussed the surgery. He then checked my genital area as he needed to make sure I had enough 'donor material' for the procedure that I had opted for. He then showed me a gallery of his work whilst explaining the procedure in a little more detail. After asking a few questions, he passed me onto someone else to book me in for surgery, and I was given the date of December 15th for my surgery, just a week after my birthday and only ten days before Christmas: what a fantastic present that was going to be.

It transpired that my surgeon's three-month wait was the wait to be initially seen, and his surgery waiting list was eight months. I went away bouncing with joy and as soon as I got home I sat down and the reality finally hit me: I was getting my surgery. I cried through sheer happiness.

I continued to bounce through life on a high for a few weeks before the police informed me that they were not continuing with my case against Eugene due to them being unable to trace the origin of the emails and the lack of fingerprints on the letters. They would however keep the case open in case Eugene slipped up in the future. My actions against Eugene some months earlier had meant I had been hassle-free and my hope now was that this state would continue.

In May, I decided on two new projects: one was to find out how diverse and accepting York was towards the LGBT community and ethnic minorities. The idea was to have couples of the same gender walk along set routes with marshals observing the public reaction, and I set that up to take place in August.

Before that though I was going to launch a transgender workshop aimed at helping other transgender people to get through day-to-day life with less hassle and stress, and helping them through the transition process via gender clinics. I planned this to launch at the end of July.

Just when everything in my life was looking rosy, I was yet again hit with a bombshell: the car failed its MOT miserably and I was left thinking, *Why me?* Why do I never get a good run without something going wrong? I certainly couldn't afford the cost of the repairs, they came to more than the car was worth, and I decided against throwing good money after bad to repeat the process the following year and applied for finance for a newer car with a better history. I must have had a decent credit rating as I got my loan and got a good car which I hoped would not cost too much in repairs over the five-year finance period that was necessary.

The workload at the forum was about to drastically increase too, with the new Lord Mayor of York naming York LGBT Forum as one of his four chosen charities of the year; that meant the fundraising done for the Lord Mayor's charities had to be done alongside our existing work, but it would also give us a huge boost in finances as well as raising our profile in and around York.

Twenty Five

Transgender workshop and the BBC

In the build-up to the transgender workshop, I found myself back at Minster FM to talk about it for radio. I went direct from a night shift, so it's a good job it wasn't television. The radio interview went very well and I pushed it via social media an awful lot, so I was just hoping that people would turn up. I was unsure how many would come; it could fall flat on its face or be standing room only.

I had lined up a couple of good friends to be the 'experts' in their field, a transgender male and a non-binary person, and I would fill the transgender female role. With the workshop, it was hard to have a set agenda or timetable without knowing who would come, so I devised a rough plan of action.

On the day itself I was picking up my good friend Tim from their house and we got stuck in traffic due to a protest march of some description, so instead of arriving early and getting everything set up, we got there just on the actual start time and had to rush around rearranging the seating and preparing the tables. Without having time to worry or wonder about people coming, nerves vanished in a haze of activity as we got the room set up just in time for the first person arriving and within minutes the room was packed.

After an excellent few hours with a roomful of people, it was safe to declare the transgender workshop an overwhelming success and plans were made to make it a quarterly event. To my knowledge, at that time, it was the first such workshop anywhere in the UK, certainly within Yorkshire, and I told the Leeds gender clinic all about it; they appeared to be very interested and asked to be kept informed about the details of the next workshop, which I had pencilled in for October.

Earlier in the year I had helped the gender clinic with an open day they had held for people on the waiting list for their first appointment, a waiting list which by now had grown from twelve months when I was on it, to about three and half years.

The day after, August 1st, Yorkshire Day, was a major fundraising event for the Lord Mayor's charities too. We had a full day of events tagged on to the end of the Great Yorkshire Fringe festival, a small version of the Edinburgh Fringe festival, and apart from selling raffle tickets and collecting money via collection buckets, we had a talent show, *York's Got Talent*, a tongue-in-cheek spin-off of *Britain's Got Talent*, and I played the role of Amanda Holden for the judging.

It was amazing fun and an all-round great day, but oh so tiring, as when that ended around 11pm I had an engagement with the Monday night karaoke at my local pub.

Through my transgender workshop, the BBC got to hear about me and my work within the transgender community and I was invited to talk live on BBC Radio York about NHS gender clinic waiting times as they were doing a special feature on it ahead of a big NHS meeting in Halifax. I was invited to talk on the morning of the meeting and then invited to the television studio over in Leeds to record something for BBC One's *Look North*, which was going to report on the meeting in Halifax.

I breezed through the live radio slot without a single nerve flickering and with an air of confidence and it was down to this that I got a call from the BBC in Leeds asking if could divert from the television studio and travel instead to the meeting in Halifax to be interviewed live on television from the meeting. I didn't need any persuading and I made it Halifax with an hour to spare despite my satnav dying on me on the outskirts of Halifax.

For early August, it was a blustery, chilly day. Wearing an overcoat was a must just to stay warm, but that wouldn't look very good on television, so for the interview the coat was left in the mobile BBC van. The interview itself went very smoothly, even better than my radio interview, and I showed no sign of any nerves during the interview.

Afterwards I chatted off camera to my interviewer who could not believe that it was my first time on television, never mind being live. After the meeting, I recorded another slot for the late news on BBC *Look North*, something like fifteen minutes, which was edited down to just thirty seconds.

For a few weeks after my television debut I was getting recognised almost everywhere I went. I was being stopped in shops and asked questions; at work, customers were making a beeline for me and chatting to me about my interview; in the street I was being looked at much more than usual, even more so than when I first trod the streets as Lisa; and in pubs I started getting a mixed reaction. Most people chatted and told me how brave they thought I was in what I was doing, but a minority were pointing and staring and away from the pub, they were shouting insults like 'Tranny' or 'Shemale'.

I think for the most part it was just the alcohol talking, but it left me knowing that some quarters of York still needed awareness of transgender people raising. Some people will never accept a transgender person, but most will once they know something about the issues transgender people face, and come to understand that a transgender person is no different to anyone else, let alone a threat to anyone.

In between all this activity I was having my hair removal sessions every two weeks ready for surgery, and facial hair removal every four weeks, and I was starting to feel the pressure of constantly being on the go. Work was hectic with a string of weeks doing night shifts, so at times I was breaking my sleep to attend the hair removal sessions, and I was getting more requests to give talks. On one day in particular, I finished a night shift at 6am and got two hours' sleep before a quick shower and heading out to give a two-hour presentation of 'Free to be me' followed by a quick lunch and a drive across town to give another two-hour 'Free to be me' presentation, before heading back home to grab a couple of hours' sleep before another night shift.

I couldn't rest on my laurels though, I had my other new project looming large: the 'Hands Together' human rights walk, to assess the diversity and acceptance of LGBT people in York. I used the City Screen cinema as the base for this, the seating area in the lounge was perfect to use as a headquarters and I paired people together and set them off along one of two routes holding hands as they walked, with two marshals following a short distance behind them. On their return, each person, the couple and marshals, would fill out a short questionnaire/feedback form so that I could evaluate the results and get an initial idea as to how diverse and accepting York was.

It was a fabulous afternoon which surpassed all expectations. We had one guy who deliberately dressed to try and get a reaction: he wore a sarong and had eyeshadow and lipstick on, despite sporting the George Michael look in terms of facial hair.

During the afternoon, I swapped and changed people around to pair together a variety of couples and in the end, the whole afternoon passed trouble-free, which was great, but better still was the reaction from the public. It became apparent from all the feedback that the negativity was aimed towards a transgender person who did not quite 'fit in', by which I mean, you could tell at a glance that she was transgender and didn't blend into the crowd. Aside from that, the remainder of the feedback was all positive, so I concluded, this time around, that York was quite diverse and accepting unless you were transgender and stood out from the crowd as such. I made a point of aiming to carry out more research from the following spring and through the summer.

Throughout all this time from starting my transition to where I currently was, I had put relationships on ice. I was constantly worrying that any man I might have got romantically involved with would only be with me as part of their fantasy of having a girlfriend with a little bit extra between her legs, and that once I went in for my surgery and that 'bit extra' was gone, they too would be gone faster than a bullet. I also forged the idea in my mind that women didn't want to get involved with me because of that bit extra between my legs. That bit extra was the cause of about 90% of the dysphoria I felt; the other 10% was down to the extremely slow growth of my breasts.

I was edging ever closer to surgery, and I still could not completely fill an 'A' cup. The gender clinic no longer did breast augmentation surgery as part and parcel of the care pathway, it was no longer a core treatment, so I was getting increasingly pained at the lack of breast development.

It was around this time, late August, that I also began to contemplate how lonely I was. I had plenty of friends but I had now been single for a good seven years and I missed cuddling up to someone and watching a film together, or going on a night out with someone special, but most of all I was missing not having a companion to chat to when life wasn't so hectic.

I gave a few more talks in the coming weeks and by mid-September I was starting to promote the next transgender workshop, and invited the Leeds gender clinic to attend. Mid-September was also when the genital hair removal was stepped up to weekly from fortnightly. If the surgical area was not fully clear of hair then surgery would be delayed. I'd waited long enough for this surgery and couldn't bear a delay, but I was assured that I would be ready in time for surgery.

I had also sorted out everything with work to finish on December 1st and use holidays to take me up to my surgery date. I had fourteen days in which to get Christmas presents bought, wrapped and delivered along with cards.

I also started to think about stockpiling non-perishable food for the period post-surgery when I wouldn't be able to carry much shopping. I was also unsure how long it would be after leaving hospital before I would be able to walk as far as the shops and back home again. It was one aspect of the whole thing that I knew precious little about and what information I did glean from others was that each person is different, healing at different rates, but by-and-large most people were walking short distances within a few days of leaving hospital, so I pinned my hopes on being able to walk to the shops within a week of leaving the hospital.

October saw me at Beninbrough Hall again, not to talk this time; it was an art project for the National Gallery called 'Portraits Untold' featuring renowned disabled artist Tanya Rabbe-Webber. She was doing a series of audience interactive portraits, and for this one she was drawing David Hoyle, one of my heroes; he was a gay icon and extremely well-known drag artist. At school, I had enjoyed art, but had been put off by low marks from my teacher. Tanya and David were amazing and

I asked a few questions during the audience participation, as well as drawing David and Tanya on a sketch pad and an IPad. The whole day restored my own belief in art being for everyone regardless of ability. Such was the impression that the 'Portraits Untold' event and Tanya had left on me, that I decided a sketch pad and other drawing materials would be packed for my stay in hospital later in the year.

Twenty Six

Counting down to surgery

Now that my hair removal sessions were weekly on a Tuesday, it meant I could go to karaoke on a Monday night; I was using my day off each week on a Tuesday for the hair removal. I was now counting down the weeks and trying to learn a new song for karaoke each week and planned to finish with 'Like a Virgin' at my final karaoke before surgery.

With my holidays from work, I had planned three celebrations: a few drinks after the Forum meeting, which fell on my actual birthday; a real bang on the Saturday which was to be the December transgender social night; and then on the Monday night, a pre-surgery/slightly late birthday karaoke bash, my final day of drinking alcohol and the night I was going sing 'Like a Virgin'.

Before then, though, was the transgender workshop again. This time two people from Leeds gender clinic came, as well as a make-up artist. Leeds gender clinic were interested in how my workshop worked as they were taking on some extra staff to combat waiting lists, and some outreach support workers. In my dialogue with the gender clinic I had been stressing that, away from the clinical side of things, many transgender people struggled with everyday life and with how society treated them, and my workshops were aimed at that side of things, something I felt the outreach support workers needed to do, and the gender clinic agreed.

After the success of the first workshop I wasn't worried about the second one, and it proved to be another huge success with standing room only and extremely positive feedback from the gender clinic. The make-up artist was another big hit, with lessons in applying make-up going down very well, and so the next workshop was booked for late January when I hoped I would be mobile enough after surgery to run the workshop.

By now I was in full flow preparing for the York LGBT Forum AGM, which was just a month away, and I was also now counting down the days to surgery rather than the weeks. I had two more weeks of taking hormones before I had to stop: it was normal practice to stop taking hormones six weeks before surgery, and for around six weeks post-surgery.

The AGM itself went without a hitch apart from Stephanie Hirst having a technical problem with her laptop for her keynote speech, but after an interlude while it was sorted out, everything flowed, and I was re-elected as transgender subgroup coordinator. My position as co-chair went unchallenged and I immediately started making plans for the following year. Stephanie Hirst was so down to earth when we met and easy to talk to, a true inspiration for any transgender person to follow, and she proved a big hit too with the LGBT community at the AGM.

Soon after the AGM I was back at the hospital for my pre-op assessment; this was basically taking my 'bloods', swabbing for MRSA, checking blood pressure, weighing and measuring me. When I was having my height measured I joked with the nurse that I hoped she wasn't measuring me for a coffin, which went down like a lead balloon. I was given some paperwork, which was a diet sheet for the day before the surgery, lots of information about the hospital, which was a private hospital that did some NHS surgery too, and a box containing two sachets of Picolax, a special laxative which was to be taken as per the instructions on my diet sheet.

Without realising it, I was suddenly just three weeks away from surgery, although I was very excited, I wasn't in the slightest bit nervous. It was almost as if everything I had gone through up to this point, the nervous appointments, the online hassle, the verbal abuse when I was just starting to transition, had used up all my nerves and anxiety. My only worry now was getting to the day of surgery in good health. I needed to avoid colds and 'flu and not be unlucky enough to break a bone or be involved in an accident of some kind.

The final week of work arrived. I had a few shifts to get through and that would be it work-wise for the rest of the year. With other people counting down to Christmas, I was making sure everybody knew that I only had a few days at work before my working year was complete. It's fair to say some work colleagues were glad to see the back of me after I was constantly reminding them I was in my final week.

On the Sunday of that week, my first of five shifts to end my year, I got a bit emotional saying goodbye to the staff I wouldn't see for a few months, and the same happened on my last shift of the week. I knew I was going to miss work, not straight away, but during the recovery from surgery, a recovery process that I had been told would be lengthy, at least ten weeks or more, and before leaving work for the last time, handing over my rota/holiday book, I wrote in the book instructions to start putting me back on the work rota from Monday 6th March. That would give me a target of returning to work just shy of twelve weeks after surgery.

My workplace sickness policy meant that I would be paid full pay for up to ten weeks, but as my sickness period would take me into a new work year, the ten-week full pay period would start again. That meant that I could in theory take up to sixteen weeks off work with full pay.

On getting home from my last shift at work, I began to feel a little under the weather and gradually got worse as the afternoon wore on. I had several engagements to attend from the following day through until the Tuesday of the next week and being ill was the last thing I needed, apart from potentially jeopardising my surgery too. I cancelled my Thursday evening and Friday engagements and took to lying in bed under the duvet, trying my best to sweat out whatever fever I had. I was feeling sorry for myself and worrying that this bout of illness could delay my surgery, the problem being that although it was a form of cold, I had a history of not recovering fully from cold or 'flu for some weeks after being well enough to resume normal duties. Basically, I could recover quite quickly from the worst of these bugs, but then struggle to shake off the last remnants of the bug or virus.

By the Monday I was feeling well enough to make it to karaoke, but before that, during the day I had my final talk prior to surgery to give, to York College. That went extremely well; it was to their newly formed LGBT group, so they were already pretty clued-up on the subject.

I had finished my hair removal in readiness for the surgery, so I could really let my hair down at karaoke that night. After being ill, I had re-planned my week to try and leave the following week free, and so after recovering from the previous night's karaoke, I went shopping for the remainder of the Christmas presents I still needed to buy. After battling through the crowds of shoppers, I made it home early evening and got all my cards written and presents wrapped that same evening. My plan was to deliver everything later that week.

Thursday was my actual birthday, the day I delivered Christmas to my family and relatives, and then we had the Forum's meeting that evening followed by a few drinks in the pub afterwards, a nice steady night one week prior becoming a virgin again, Saturday would be the day when I had my last big 'blow' before the surgery.

I had deliberately moved forward the transgender social night by a week to accommodate my own attendance as the social was not yet at the stage where it would still be able to run without me being there, and I had doubled it up with my birthday celebrations which I was doing in three parts, the social night being the main one for letting my hair down. It was well attended and Tim almost constantly kept me supplied with cocktails, on top of what we were drinking anyway, and for a change I spent most of the night dancing. I never normally dance too much due to having two left feet, but the drink was making me do things I didn't normally do.

It was a great night and I felt fine when leaving the pub, but that fresh winter air hit me almost instantly and I found myself 'wobbling' the few hundred yards to the taxi rank. I recall standing in the queue but wobbling so much that I was bumping into those in front of me and then wobbling backwards into those queuing behind me. I needed some support to remain standing upright, so with my completely irrational thinking, I decided to walk to the train station for a taxi, a walk of half a mile, but it did have a rail at the taxi rank that I could prop myself up on.

At 3am there was never much traffic on the roads, which was a good job: once I had staggered over the river bridge, I fell into the road. After picking myself up and dusting myself down, I walked, or rather stumbled, another fifty yards or so before I decided to try out being horizontal once more, this time it was the pavement that greeted me rather than the road, and once again I got up quickly and staggered further along the path. I made it as far as an arch that crossed both the pavement and road, a mere three hundred yards from the train station before my face said hello to the footpath again. This time, though, I decided I was too tired to get up again, I decided that I would go to sleep right there on the wet footpath.

Sometime later some young adults came across me laid on the floor and tried to rouse me from my slumber, I heard one of them on their phone asking for an ambulance, that was when I finally opened my eyes and tried to stand up. I certainly didn't need an ambulance. The group who had found me were right to be concerned, I could have been out cold or suffering concussion, but I was fine, apart from needing to sleep, and so I thanked them for their concern and began my journey towards the train station. They did accompany me all the way, helping to keep me on my feet, and I wished that I had caught their names to thank them properly later, but they made sure I got a taxi at the train station, and the taxi driver made sure I got inside my house before leaving.

Sunday was a day of rest, I woke up feeling fine, no sign of a hangover, just overly tired, and I didn't feel like doing anything apart from relaxing in front of the television, though I did begin to pack a suitcase of things I would need in hospital.

I got an early night ahead of going back to the hospital Monday morning for my blood to be taken so that it could be cross-matched in case I needed a transfusion for any reason during my operation. Throughout my appointment at the hospital I was hiding my cough and trying not show that I was still getting over the after-effects of the bug that I had come down with just over a week earlier. I didn't want to give them any reason to postpone my surgery.

Karaoke that night was emotional: it was my final one before surgery and I was not sure for how long I would be unable to go to karaoke after my surgery. It wasn't a night for drinking too much alcohol, I was now too close to surgery and really shouldn't even have been drinking at that stage, so I took it steady. I sang my usual few songs before singing Madonna's 'Like a Virgin', and then having a cry after singing it. I had been saying for months that my surgery would in effect make me a virgin once again, so it seemed appropriate to sing that song.

Tuesday, two days before the surgery that would change my life and body, I did the last of my shopping. Food was the mainstay, stockpiling supplies that were non-perishable, and I had a Chinese takeaway for tea, my last proper meal. Amazingly, despite being just days away from the operation to save my life, the operation that would see my dysphoria vanish and give me a chance to finally start living my life rather than just existing from day to day, I still showed no sign of getting nervous.

Next morning I was onto the diet sheet from the hospital, I was awake early and at 7.30am I took the first sachet of Picolax. It tasted absolutely disgusting and nearly made me throw up. I had no idea how long it would take to work, so I continued by making my breakfast, a meal I normally skipped but given the diet sheet, I was taking advantage of every opportunity to eat what I was allowed.

Breakfast was a single poached egg on a slice of toast with a cup of tea and I then caught up with emails, played a game on the computer and made a phone call to my dad to remind him about picking me up the following morning around 9am.

Around 9.30am the Picolax began to work and I dashed to the loo, spending the next forty-five minutes back and forth to the loo before things settled down. I even joked on Facebook that today was a day for not wearing knickers. 10.30am and I was allowed my mid-morning cup of tea, this diet sheet even instructed when and what I could drink, as well as what I could eat. During that mid-morning cuppa, I got my first sign of nerves: butterflies in my stomach. It felt like the diet combined with the bowel movements were finally hitting home that my life was about to change forever.

I had two eggs left that would go off if not eaten, so my lunch at midday was two poached eggs on two slices of toast, my final solid food, and of course a cup of tea, my final cuppa.

After lunch, I finished packing my suitcase, apart from the essentials that I would need the next morning. All too soon it was time for the second sachet of Picolax. I added a drop of orange juice to take the edge off the taste, and then I figured I had time to wash my car. I got as far as filling a bucket with warm water before a familiar feeling had me running to the loo. The diet sheet said to drink plenty of water until bowel movements had ceased. The way it seemed to me was that every time I had a drink of water, five minutes later I was sat on the loo and it continued like that for the rest of the day.

Late afternoon, I got a call from the hospital asking if it was possible for me to be there at 9am, they had brought my operation forward to 11am from 2pm. Naturally, I said yes before checking if my dad could take me earlier than planned, but he was fine with it.

With all the rushing to the loo, I had got through two full rolls of toilet paper and was developing a headache through dehydration, but I couldn't take any medication without consulting the hospital, so I just put up with it. At 7pm I was allowed a meat extract drink for supper, which tasted surprisingly nice, and with bowel movements slowing down by 9pm I went to bed soon after. I couldn't sleep, I was far too excited.

Twenty Seven

Authentic at last

After an interrupted night's sleep the alarm clock roused me properly at 5am. Without thinking I made a cup of tea out of habit before realising I was only allowed a small glass of water. Good job I didn't drink the tea, I don't know what would have happened or if the hospital would know, but I figured there was a good reason behind not allowing a cup of tea, so it was poured down the plughole.

After showering, I dressed and finished packing the suitcase, and the previous day's butterflies had vanished. I was looking forward to getting to hospital. I had a last cigarette just to settle me down while I waited for my dad to arrive and then with his car loaded with my suitcase, we set off in plenty of time on the forty-minute drive to my home for the next week, hospital.

I sat in the reception area next to the free drinks machine watching a progression of people pass by, grab a drink and move on. I was desperate for a nice hot drink. By now, I had a pounding headache and my lips were extremely dry. It was as though everyone was teasing me, torturing me, knowing I couldn't have a nice hot cuppa.

Finally, a nurse arrived, called out my name, and took me to my temporary room – my own room wouldn't be ready until 10am – and with me settled in the room, my dad went home. I didn't unpack my case, I was hoping I would be moved to my own room before I went down to theatre.

I was just in the middle of broadcasting live on Facebook, telling any viewers about my room and how I thought the day was going to pan out, when the anaesthetist arrived to check my details and go through the procedure with me. He asked how I was feeling and I told him that, apart from the banging headache, I was excited. He put on my notes for the ward nurse to allow me to have half a cup of water at 10am.

Soon after that, Mr Church, my surgeon, arrived. We had a chat and I signed the consent forms. Still no sign of being nervous or apprehensive, in fact I was so excited that I was starting feel emotional, emotional in that I knew in a few short hours my dysphoria would be gone and I would finally feel authentic. Time was now ticking round ever so slowly, watching the clock wasn't helping, but it finally edged towards 10am and I was collected and taken to my actual room, my home for the next seven days. I unpacked my case and knowing I would be stuck in bed for four or five days, I made sure that everything I thought I would need was close at hand.

I had been warned many times that whilst in hospital, boredom was the biggest issue, so I had puzzle books, sketch pad, phone charger and a selfie stick. I wasn't planning on taking any selfies, it was so I could extend it to reach beyond the limits of my arms.

I had just got everything where I wanted it when the nurse came with my water, and the dreaded enema. After the previous day, I had wondered if there was anything else left inside me to be cleared out, but within ten minutes the enema had done its job.

I was back on Facebook Live giving an update, and using it as a way to pass time until just after 11am, when two nurses came into my room. I put on my dressing gown and slippers and we walked to the anaesthesia room next to the operating theatre.

I was asked to confirm my name and date of birth, and to confirm the procedure I was about to have, and then I disrobed and removed my slippers, which were taken back to my room and I got onto the bed. A cannula was inserted into my left hand and I was asked a question as a liquid was injected through the cannula. I could feel my feet and then my legs go to sleep and that feeling crept up my body. I didn't get to answer the question before I was out cold.

The next thing I remember was waking up in my room, disorientated and very sleepy. I got as far as posting a status on Facebook, 'I am a Virgin again', and then going to sleep for another couple of hours. When my eyes opened again I turned on the television with the intention of watching my soaps, but as the credits started rolling for *Emmerdale*, my eyes closed again, and I continued to drift in and out of sleep for the next few hours.

I woke up properly around midnight. I was aware of a new feeling, one that I had never experienced before: it was a feeling of total and utter contentment. I had been happy and joyous before, but this was a new feeling, a feeling of being comfortable within my own body, at ease with myself. I was so happy that I had tears rolling down my face. A nurse was walking past my room, the door was propped slightly open, and she popped in to see if I was OK. I told her through the tears of joy that I felt fantastic but could murder a hot drink. Ten minutes later I had a cup of tea at my bedside, it was in a spill-proof beaker that toddlers use, but given that I was flat on my back, it was a good thing; I just wanted that hot drink.

The next few hours followed a similar pattern of one or two hours' sleep and a cup of tea, the nurse coming in every couple of hours and taking my blood pressure and monitoring my breathing, and every four hours my drip was changed over to a liquid antibiotic which would run through in about fifteen minutes and then I would be hooked back up to the other drip which had previously been attached. Strangely through all this I didn't feel hungry until 7am, but it was another hour or so before breakfast.

I was using Facebook Live as a way to converse with friends rather than post status updates, and I found myself blown away by all the support and love I was getting from people watching my live blogs. It wasn't just friends, it was complete strangers too, that morning I was live at 4am and again at 7am while waiting for breakfast, and both times my live audience had me in tears, I just couldn't get my head round the sheer level of support, love and goodwill messages I was getting.

Breakfast was two slices of toast, which took me a while to eat. I was still flat on my back and swallowing wasn't easy; it was compounded by a sore throat from the tubes that were in my mouth during surgery. Despite that, toast had never tasted so nice, and just two slices filled me up.

I was aware from about 4am onwards of backache slowly building and trapped wind too, and both were getting steadily worse throughout the morning. I had been told that one feature of this surgery was horrendous trapped wind and sometimes backache too, but this pain I was feeling was going way beyond anything I had felt before when I had suffered trapped wind, and the backache was making things worse. The painkillers I was being given were taking the edge off the backache, as well as leaving me pain-free in the surgery area, but they were doing nothing to alleviate the trapped wind.

Soon after breakfast, with me now reduced to tears with the back pain and what I was now describing as a hurricane-force trapped wind, I was given an extra strong painkiller and had some Buscopan injected through the cannula to relieve the wind. I was having difficulty breathing properly and the slight cough that I had gone into hospital with, a throwback to that bug or virus a couple of weeks earlier, had got significantly worse, compounded by the very tight corset bandage that I was wearing post-surgery.

The Buscopan alleviated my symptoms by the time visiting hours arrived. I had managed lunch, just a sandwich, and being in much less pain I was looking forward to having some visitors. My overall feeling was one of tiredness, all the sleep I had managed was in spells of one or two hours at a time, and aside from the cough and trapped wind, I couldn't feel any pain from the surgery area except when I had to roll onto my side, either for the dressing to be changed or to try and ease the wind problem, though I couldn't stay on my side for longer than about five minutes.

For my first afternoon after the surgery, it went quite quickly, helped by having visitors and going live on Facebook. Tea was nice too, it was the first time I had got away from bread, I chose cottage pie with vegetables, and it was extremely tasty and filling, a million miles away from what other people had told me about hospital food.

By late evening it was the corset giving me the most pain. It was just so tight and made taking deep breaths quite hard. It was designed to be tight, my surgeon had a slightly different technique which involved tightly packing the area around the wound to keep swelling down to a minimum, so it really was a case of no pain no gain where the corset was concerned.

Another night of interrupted sleep followed, and during the night I had an oxygen tube attached to aid my breathing and to keep my oxygen saturation levels up and by morning I was quite perky, probably aided by the strong painkillers, but I was looking forward to a better day thinking the trapped wind issue was over and done with. More good news came when the nurse changed my dressing. She told me that after breakfast I could raise the top third of my bed to allow me to be at a forty-five-degree angle. Though still confined to bed, at least I was no longer going to be flat on my back.

Through all that I had gone through so far in my recovery, albeit still less than two days since the operation, I had felt no dysphoria but I was highly emotional, helped in part by my own feeling of finally being complete and authentic, but also by the huge amount of support and well wishes that had completely overwhelmed me, very often reducing me to tears when doing live broadcasts on Facebook.

Twenty Eight

Recovery in hospital

I was still quite euphoric about finally having had my surgery, and that I had come through it without any complications. I had even managed to hide my cough to a large degree, the cough I had been carrying ever since I had been hit by a bug or virus a couple of weeks before my surgery. That came back to bite me on the arse later that second day.

During the course of Saturday, I enjoyed a lovely lunch and was very upbeat and perky, even laughing and joking with the staff and nurses whenever they came to my room. I had a couple of visitors after lunch, and I was mightily relieved that they came, it was so nice to see friends in the flesh, but once they had gone, my cough started to worsen. In effect my immune system was diluted: it was fighting the wound from surgery, trying to heal it, and so the chest infection, which had been almost dormant apart from that niggling cough, returned.

During surgery, pipes are inserted into the mouth and down the throat, and that allowed phlegm to build up. Late afternoon

I was starting to feel decidedly worse and went downhill rapidly. Tea arrived; I had ordered poached haddock with all the trimmings, but as lovely as it looked, I managed to eat just one slice of carrot before pushing it away. I was struggling to breathe and swallow, I was coughing much more and I was feeling very hot, to compound all that, the trapped wind had returned with a vengeance. I rang the bell for the nurse with tears starting to run down my face.

My blood pressure was sky-high and oxygen levels very low, so I was put onto an oxygen mask and had an injection, as well as an antibiotic drip and a fresh dose of Buscopan. The member of staff who came to collect my lunch, seeing that I had not touched it, made me a ham sandwich and put it in the fridge in case I got hungry later, and brought me a fresh pot of tea.

Within a few hours, I was wind-free and feeling a little better. The restrictive corset had been loosened a little to aid my breathing, but through all this I felt completely exhausted, yet try as I might, I could not manage more than an hour's sleep. Wide awake at 10pm, I had the sandwich that had been kept for me. I was quite perky again after going downhill so rapidly; despite my perkiness though, I was kept on oxygen and had regular medication to combat the infection that I had carried into hospital.

By midnight I asked for something to help me sleep. I was so shattered and needed more than just one or two hours' sleep. I needed a full night to get the rest I needed and to allow my body to fight the infection. I woke on day three post-surgery around 7am after the best night's sleep I had managed in nearly two weeks. I felt refreshed and invigorated, and my breathing was much better, so much so that I came off the oxygen and I was almost immediately complaining that the cannula was itchy and irritating. I wanted it taking out, as to my knowledge it had now served its purpose, but it stayed in.

I was feeling very little pain from the surgery area, just a dull ache, and I was looking forward to seeing visitors. It felt like this was the day that my recovery would start in earnest and get easier. It was Sunday and I was already asking about getting out of bed and into the reclining chair at my bedside. I wasn't scheduled to leave bed rest until Tuesday and I was told sympathetically that I had to stay in bed.

I only went live on Facebook once on the Sunday, but all my viewers could see how happy I was and the change within me in just one day. Some could hardly believe that I had undergone major surgery just three days earlier. I think my relatively pain-free state in the surgery area throughout my time in hospital was mostly down to the painkillers, I certainly knew when I had taken them as I was quite giddy for a short time after each dose.

What followed though was yet another night of broken sleep, managing at the most just two hours at a time. Despite that I awoke on Monday morning very chirpy and was telling jokes to the staff who had all been fantastic with me, making me feel like I was in the Hilton Hotel rather than in hospital. I felt that I was ahead of schedule in my recovery, and Monday morning saw Mr Church visit me shortly after breakfast. He was very pleased with my progress and said the cannula could come out, and followed that by telling me he'd send a nurse along to get me out of bed and into the chair for thirty minutes or so.

Instantly the tears rolled down my face. It was such a huge moment for me, I was overwhelmed with sheer ecstasy. I had set myself little goals to aim for whilst in hospital; the first big one was getting out of bed, and here I was, about to achieve that goal a day ahead of schedule. The raw emotion just flowed from me. When the nurse had taken out the cannula, she helped me to get out of bed and onto my feet. I was extremely wobbly at first, but only had a few steps to take to reach the chair. All through this, the tears of joy were running down my face; it felt like the first steps towards being discharged from hospital.

Once in the chair I was very comfortable and in even less pain, which I couldn't understand, as instead of being laid across the padding around the surgery area, I was now sat on it, so in theory had all my weight pressing down on it. Therefore, it should have caused more discomfort and pain, but it didn't. I went straight onto Facebook Live, and people watching could see the raw emotions I was going through, the tears, the laughter, the puffy eyes and the euphoria. It was like I had been handcuffed to the bed, like someone had strapped me to a rack ready to be stretched, then maybe hung drawn and quartered, and that's about what I told my watching audience, adding that a part of me had escaped being hung, but had been drawn and quartered, such was my sense of humour.

At last I was out of bed, and a new goal for that day was to walk to my bathroom and take care of washing myself, and brushing my teeth for the first time since the morning of my surgery. I was really looking forward to that because my mouth felt like a sewer. Another goal for the day was to use the toilet. My urine was taken care of via the catheter, but at some stage I would need to poo. My final goal of that day was to walk out of my room and see the big wide world, well, at least see along the corridor.

Almost an hour passed before a nurse popped in to see how I was, asking if I needed to lay down again. My reply was curt, 'I might only be out of bed on remand, but I'm not going back before I've had a walk outside of my room.' She laughed and replied with, 'Well don't venture out of your room without one of us in case you need some help.'

Over the next couple of hours, I achieved my goals for the day apart from going outside my room. It was now visiting time, so I decided to wait for visitors. It had reached 5pm and teatime and no sign of anyone visiting me. I had been very bored at times during my confinement to bed, and now my first day out of bed had descended into further extreme boredom. Television was not that good, most good shows were aired in the evening. I had sketched an outline of my view from the window, and done some puzzles, but I really needed interaction with people. My internet connection that day was patchy, so I couldn't do much online and I was becoming tetchy. I had a new-found freedom, however I hadn't exercised it yet.

Straight after tea, I left my room, carrying my catheter bag. I hadn't called for any aid; by now, I was steady on my feet, my walk was very slow though. I was still quite weak and with all my padding round the surgery area, I was waddling rather than walking. I went live on Facebook whilst walking along the corridor. I managed to waddle along towards the operating theatre and as I made it to the staff nurse's desk, she said, 'What are you doing walking outside your room?'

I responded with, 'Just having a walk'.

The reply I got was, 'You should stay in your room. What if you have a fall?'

'What if I fall in my room but can't reach my alarm bell? Out here if I fall, someone will notice me much sooner,' I responded.

'Hmm, well, I can't argue with that; just be careful and take it easy,' the staff nurse replied.

'Oh, don't worry, I will, I'm building up towards going down to reception tomorrow for a cappuccino from the drinks machine.'

Despite my new-found mobility, I endured another night of interrupted sleep and I awoke to find I had no internet. There were builders on the hospital site extending the facilities and car park and it turned out that they had severed the cable to the hospital Wi-Fi. The hospital was surrounded by woodland which also meant I had no O2 cloud coverage, meaning no internet and a very patchy telephone connection. I could no longer coordinate visitors.

I made a couple of trips downstairs to the drinks machine during the day, but boredom was now a big factor. The staff at the hospital were utterly fantastic, I felt like royalty, but they still had their jobs to do, and I needed to interact with people. With no internet, I could not get onto social media or broadcast live, and I had no visitors for the rest of my stay in hospital. Each day now was following a pattern of interrupted nights and boredom, but I was rapidly improving from the surgery.

The day before I was due to be discharged, the pack inside my new vagina was due to be removed. That meant a good long soak in a warm bath to loosen the pack and any dried blood. It was such a relief to have the corset removed and get into a bath. After a good long soak in the bath, it was time to lie on the bed for the nurse to remove the pack. I was extremely nervous about the pack coming out, I had heard that it hurts. Fortunately, I had taken my latest dose of painkillers just before getting into the bath. The nurse talked me through the procedure and I relaxed as best I could before giving the nurse the go-ahead to start.

As the pack started to come out, I felt as though my insides were being torn out of me, it was quite painful and with the nurse going nice and slow it was prolonged, but I had been told the procedure should not be rushed, so I simply gritted my teeth and closed my eyes as it felt like a house brick was being pulled through the eye of a needle. Once the pack was out, I wiped my new vagina clean, dried it off and for the first time since becoming a virgin, I could wear my own knickers. Admittedly, they were two sizes too big, but I had been told to buy larger knickers for the first weeks of the recovery, and of course I had to wear a sanitary towel too.

For the first time in my life I knew how a woman felt during her period. I could never experience the pain involved, but I quickly found out exactly how uncomfortable sanitary towels were: it was like sitting on a pebble.

I still had the catheter attached, but without the tight corset holding it in place, I could feel every movement: when I walked, or rather, waddled, I could feel the catheter, and if I coughed, I felt it. It was a huge moment having the pack taken out, but it came with pain. I now had a constant dull ache, but the painkillers made life quite pleasant and I had a new mobility, I was walking freely and able to breathe properly. I was now counting down the hours until I could go home.

As each nurse finished their shift, if they were going off duty until after my release from hospital, they were coming in to my room and spending a few minutes with me, wishing me a merry Christmas, and good luck for my recovery and new life. I found that every single member of the hospital team oozed kindness and compassion and each one treated me with the utmost dignity and respect. It really did feel more like a five-star hotel, and I knew that the following day, whilst I would be overjoyed to be going home, it would be a wrench leaving behind such a wonderful group of people.

Twenty Nine

Home for Christmas

Thursday 22nd December 2016 was a day I will never forget. One week after my surgery, and after a sleepless night, I was dressed in an ankle-length dress and slippers! I was eager for the clock to tick round and signal my release, it was still only 7am though. I only had the television for company now because I had packed everything away ready for my dad collecting me and taking me home.

I had taken some sanitary towels into hospital with me, as advised by them, and was now wearing one of them. I had grown tired of seeing the countless television adverts for 'Always Ultra, with wings' and foolishly thought they would be fine for me to wear for the next week or so while the wounds healed and stopped weeping blood or puss. By the time I had eaten my breakfast at 8am, I was getting very uncomfortable. I found it was hurting whenever my legs moved until finally it dawned on me that ultra-thin sanitary towels were not designed for use next to raw, sore, healing skin. I had a couple of maternity towels left, so I replaced the Always Ultra with a maternity towel, the relief was almost instant.

I was due to be discharged between 9.30am and 10am. I couldn't wait to get home and have access to the internet again, to be in familiar surroundings, but most of all, to have my own comfy bed again. I was hoping my own bed would bring an end to the broken sleep I had endured throughout my hospital stay.

I had a steady flow of visitors that morning, nursing staff coming to say goodbye to me, and by the time of my discharge, the tears were again streaming down my face, they were tears of joy at going home, but also tears tinged with sadness. I had grown fond of the people at the hospital, we had struck up a rapport and it was gut-wrenching leaving them behind.

Going out to my dad's car, I was waddling slowly, slightly unsteady on my feet. I had kept my slippers on purely for comfort, and told my dad I needed to stop off at a shop on the way home to get some essentials. I needed bread and sanitary towels. I had lots of soya milk, but needed some eggs and sausages too.

Getting into the car wasn't the easiest of operations. I used my arms to support most of my weight as I swivelled into the seat, and then used my hands to lift myself off the car seat slightly so the uneven road with all its bumps and potholes didn't hurt too much. It was an uncomfortable ride home. Stopping off at a shop, I wandered round the shop and never gave a moment's thought as to what other shoppers might think as I went about my shopping in my slippers.

At home, my dad carried my suitcase into the house and then left. I had the joy of carting it upstairs, and hadn't thought about how much it weighed; it was much heavier than when I went into hospital because of all the baskets of fruit and chocolates that my visitors had brought into hospital for me. I struggled a bit getting my case upstairs and into my room, and

I was, by now, in a fair amount of pain too. My last painkillers taken at hospital had worn off and each movement I made was sending a vibration-like sensation along the catheter. It was an unpleasant feeling, and I was almost at bursting point with the need to drain the catheter.

The catheter was to stay in situ for just over two weeks. Overnight I would have to attach it to a drainage bag, but during the day the pipe would be strapped to my thigh and I would have to empty the catheter into the toilet using the 'flip-flow' mechanism.

As I placed my suitcase on the bed, ready to unpack it, the strain of carrying it upstairs and then lifting it onto the bed made the sensation of wanting the loo unbearable, and I rushed into the bathroom to drain the catheter. As I opened the flip-flow valve and relaxed, I felt some urine flow down the outside of the catheter tube. The main reason for keeping the catheter in situ for so long was to reduce the possibility of getting a urinary tract infection, so the feeling of urine passing down my urinary tract outside the catheter tube had me worried.

I cleaned the area as best I could but couldn't get my mind off the thought of what would happen next time I had to drain the catheter. I had not experienced that problem at the hospital, but also, I hadn't reached a point where I was bursting for the loo in hospital either.

I got unpacked and laid out everything I thought I would need in easy reach, and then made a cup of tea and attempted to sit at my computer. It was a massive failure, it hurt far too much, I couldn't yet sit completely upright, so I made do with my mobile phone and went live on Facebook. It was another extremely emotional live broadcast, reconnecting with my followers and describing the past few days as well as letting them all know that I was back home in familiar surroundings and in need of visitors. Throughout the live broadcast, tears flowed, they were euphoric tears, and partly brought on by my viewers commenting on how well I looked and how happy they were to see me safe and well.

I laid on top of my bed out of breath, my energy levels were well below what they were before the surgery, I was finding it hard adjusting to life outside the hospital, the past week I had been waited on hand and foot, but now I was fending for myself, and I didn't have a nice comfy chair to relax in. I had heard via other people who had gone through the same surgery that the recovery period was all about listening to your body, resting when tired, sleeping when needing to, and generally taking things steady. It reached late afternoon before it dawned on me that lunch was not being served unless I got up and made it myself.

I had been waited on hand and foot in hospital and got so used to it that having to cook for myself came as a bit of a culture shock. A sausage sandwich later and I was already thinking about ordering a Chinese takeaway for tea, a way of celebrating being home again.

Brian, my co-chair at the York LGBT Forum, came to see me on my first afternoon at home. I had sent him a text with a couple of things I needed from the shops, and we had a good long chat. Brian knew that I would be alone on Christmas Day, and like the previous year, he offered me the option to spend the day at his house with his partner and another friend of theirs.

That night, I went to sleep quite late, having spent much of the day snoozing. I was so glad to be in own comfy bed but I hadn't reckoned with the 'power of the catheter'. I was looking forward to a good night of solid sleep now that I had a double bed to sprawl out in, but found that each time I changed position in bed, the catheter drainage tube would kink and cause a pressure build-up. I could manage to fall asleep on my side with the aid of a cushion to support my leg or knee, but any movement was painful enough to wake me up. Eventually, being so exhausted, I would drop into a deep sleep, only to be awoken by the pressure build-up from the kinked tube, and I would have to untangle the drainage tube to allow my bladder to drain.

I gave up trying to sleep at 3am, just five hours after going to bed. Another Facebook Live broadcast later and I was planning on a shower and then a walk. Normally a shower followed by a walk would have taken about an hour from showering to walking, but I couldn't carry much, so my shower supplies like shampoo and such were carried the very short journey along the landing, in two trips, and then I had to set everything up in easy reach to avoid bending too much whilst in the shower.

That first shower since surgery was not as easy as I thought. The catheter had to be unstrapped from my thigh because the strap itself was not waterproof; that meant the catheter would be left dangling between my legs during the shower and each time the catheter swung with my movements, I felt a strange tingle in my bladder, not a pleasant tingle, but one that caused a slight sensation of pain, mild, but enough to be felt.

In all, from preparing to shower, to getting out of the shower, forty-five minutes had passed. Another hour later and I had dried off, got dressed and taken my first painkillers of the day, with a cup of tea and a light breakfast.

The closest shop to my house was a five-minute walk, about 800 yards, a journey I thought would be beyond my capabilities, but I set off at a slow, steady pace. It was mostly downhill towards that shop, and I reached around 200 yards from the shop before I stopped. I was completely out of breath and nearly exhausted and it had taken me fifteen minutes, with the return walk back home still to come and mostly uphill. I decided to broadcast live on Facebook during my slow walk back home, showing my audience how I was coping and how much effort went into something simple like a short walk. The return journey to my house took me over twenty minutes.

My first full day at home followed a path of watching television, broadcasting on Facebook and eating, at least during the times I could keep my eyes open. Brian came around to collect my doctor's note signing me off work for six weeks, and took it into work for me. Brian was a solid rock for me, always there if I needed anyone, and already on day one after my release from hospital, I found myself getting bored quickly and in need of visitors.

I couldn't drive my car yet; I was told I could only drive when I was pain-free, could operate the foot pedals properly and look over my shoulder, and they estimated that would be at least four weeks after surgery, and usually took six weeks.

The only pain I felt was a dull ache, more of a nuisance than a real pain. I was planning a second walk: the recovery process was geared towards being as mobile as possible, rather than lying in bed letting the wounds heal, but it was winter, it was very cold and there was a strong wind blowing with a threat of rain too. I hated the cold weather, winter was my least favourite season, and I decided to stay indoors.

That night, I hoped for a good sleep, but my routine since the day before surgery was one of broken sleep, and so it followed that I had another poor night in bed. It had rained most of the night and daybreak arrived with the weather improving slightly, scattered heavy showers. With that in mind I waited for a break in the clouds before heading out for a walk. This time I was determined to reach the shops, and I made it to a shop about half a mile from my house before the clouds drifted over on the wind and the heavens opened. I only needed bread and milk from the shop, but I wandered up and down every aisle hoping the rain would stop.

I caught a break in the cloud and set off back home, moving a little quicker than the previous day. I had done the one-mile round trip and made it home cold but dry, in slightly less time than it had taken me the day before.

It was Christmas Eve and I had no shortage of visitors, I was also pain-free, totally pain-free, but I kept up with taking my painkillers because I worried that they were keeping pain at bay and I would feel the pain if I stopped taking them. I still couldn't manage to sit upright properly, let alone sit at my computer, so I continued broadcasting live on Facebook to a growing audience, and describing how I felt and I started a series of video blogs about the lead-up to surgery and the recovery.

As much as I wanted a drink to toast Christmas, I wasn't allowed alcohol, so at midnight I toasted Christmas with a cup of tea and followed it with the best night's sleep I had managed unaided by sleeping pills since a couple of days prior to my surgery and I woke up feeling fully refreshed and raring to go on Christmas morning.

I kept up my daily routine of going for a walk, but with a long day ahead of me, I limited my walk to just ten minutes. All too soon it was nearing lunchtime and Brian came around to pick me up in his car to take me to his house for the day. Armed with a travel pillow to use as a cushion, the short drive was easy and I settled into a comfy chair that I could slightly lie back in.

Eating Christmas dinner was a different matter, I ended up having to sit in Brian's computer chair with a travel pillow for support and after the first course I finally got comfortable and enjoyed one of the most delicious Christmas dinners that I had eaten in a long time. It was a traditional Christmas dinner, turkey with all the trimmings, Brian's partner was certainly a great cook, and I could not have wished to spend the day in more pleasant company. Time flew by and before I knew it, Brian had taken me home again and I was back into my care routine, ready to watch television in bed whilst propped up on my pillows.

Yet another night of interrupted sleep followed. I was starting to think that I only got a proper sleep when I was too exhausted to wake up. Boxing Day was day eleven post-surgery, and I never felt so alone as I was that day, the whole day passed with no visitors, no one-to-one human interaction, and it was the first day of total boredom, I got so down and felt so sorry for myself that I just vegetated all day on my bed, watching old movies and catching an hour or two of sleep here and there. I did manage the entire daytime without taking any painkillers, but took some before trying to get some sleep. I had stayed almost pain-free all day, apart from a dull ache, but I was starting to see hair regrowth, having shaved for surgery, and this was just reaching that irritable length that gets incredibly itchy.

What little swelling I had from the surgery was now starting to ease too, and the first of my stitches were starting to dissolve. With the stitches protruding out from the skin because of the reduction in swelling, they were starting to snag in my knickers and cause some discomfort, especially when combined with the sanitary towels.

Thirty

Listening to my body

During the next few days I was conscious of trying not to overdo things. I was still quite fragile and building up my strength was a priority, so I settled into a daily routine of walking to the shops and staying as mobile as I could whilst listening to what my body was telling me.

I had given up on sleeping properly like a normal person; instead I took powernaps as and when I felt tired and I would lie down on the bed when I felt my energy levels were low. Pain-wise I just had a constant dull ache, and most of my discomfort was coming from the catheter.

The week whilst I had been in hospital, none of my housemates in the house-share had put the dustbins or recycling out for collection. Christmas week saw no collections, even refuse collectors got time off at Christmas, but that meant that our bins were overflowing with another week to wait before the next refuse collection.

By now my poor little car had been stood idle for two weeks

and with it being winter, I was worrying that the brakes might seize up, or the battery would be flat. I decided to start the car with a view to just letting the engine tick over for a few minutes; it was something I could manage without getting into the car. I got adventurous though and with the aid of a cushion I sat in the car. Despite some pain, I reversed the car off the drive and back into its parking spot. The brakes worked fine, but I realised I couldn't yet drive the car, I was only thirteen days' post-surgery, and the strain on my stomach area caused me to dash to the toilet to drain the catheter. That catheter was fast becoming the bane of my life.

Each day I was taking photographs of the surgery area to keep a record of how it was healing, and because I could not bend far enough to see the area without a mirror. It was beginning to look a lot better by this stage; much of the swelling had gone down and the redness was fading away, but the stitches were getting more prominent and catching on clothing.

It seemed that I could do a fair bit of walking for two days, and suffer with pain the third day, so, listening to my body, I cut back the distance I was walking each day, and found that just a mile per day was enough to keep me mobile and active, yet keep the pain at bay. Despite everything, I felt that I was ahead of schedule with my recovery; it looked like it was going too well, problem-free, virtually pain-free, the only thing bothering me was the catheter.

In the post-Christmas, pre-New Year period, I had a steady stream of visitors to keep me company and keep my boredom levels under control but I was not looking forward to people returning to work after the festive season. I feared my visitors would dry up and that I would get extremely bored, the danger of that being I could easily become depressed.

New Year's Eve was a landmark day. My usual routine when I first woke up was to put the kettle on and lie back down on the bed whilst waiting for it to boil, but for some reason that day I placed a travel pillow on my computer chair and sat on that; for the first time since my surgery I found that I could sit in relative comfort at my computer.

Filled with that new-found confidence, after showering and having breakfast, I decided to try the travel pillow in my car. I was in a 'cannot be bothered' mood and didn't feel like walking to the shops, so I was hoping that I could sit in some degree of comfort in the car and maybe even drive to the shops. I cautiously sat on the travel pillow and practised using the foot pedals; with a little bit of trepidation, I put the key in the ignition and started the engine.

I was in a little bit of pain, not enough to stop me from engaging reverse gear and driving away. I drove to the garage nearby, a short drive, but I found it far enough for my first drive. After buying some provisions, I drove the car home and beamed with delight at my achievement: just sixteen days after having major surgery, I had reached one of my goals and driven the car, I was so proud of that milestone that I broadcast live on Facebook.

Of course, I suffered the next day; the dull ache was painful enough to have me back on painkillers all day and I did fear that I had overdone it and possibly caused a complication. That fear was compounded by noticing the urine in my overnight drainage bag was discoloured; it had a red tinge and what looked like clumps of tissue.

In the daytime, with the drainage bag detached and using the flip-flow when I felt the need to use the toilet, I discovered that I was going more often, and far less urine was coming out, and feeling rather tired I attached the overnight bag so that I could try and get an afternoon sleep. I woke up to find the drainage tube was full of what appeared to be clotted blood and tissue. It was almost blocked, and I was panicking. My first thought was to phone the hospital, but I worried that they would want me to go to the hospital, and it was New Year's Day, my only choice would have been a taxi, and that would cost me an arm and a leg due to the distance and the fact that the rates for taxis go up staggeringly for public holidays.

I tried googling the problem, and that, coupled with what others on Facebook had told me from their own experience, made me realise it was scar tissue and quite normal. I didn't stop worrying about it, but I left it overnight to see what happened, and sure enough, the next morning everything looked fine again.

The next couple of days I didn't even think about using the car, I didn't fancy another full day of suffering just because I got too lazy to walk.

On the day before the recycling was due to be collected, I asked my house mates to take out the four recycling boxes. It had been a month since we had them emptied, and they were overflowing, we just couldn't leave it for another two weeks. The following morning, I awoke to find that I may as well have been talking to a brick wall. I caught one house mate before he left to go to work and asked him to take out the recycling, 'I'll be home by 2pm, I'll do it then,' was his response.

'That's too late, they come during the morning,' I responded.

'Oh, well, I haven't got time then,' he said.

An hour later he left for work. To say I was fuming was an understatement.

I managed to take out the plastics and the paper recycling, and then tried the other two, which had glass and metal in them. I pushed them both down the couple of steps and then tried to push them along the garden path with a sweeping brush. Thirty minutes later and severely out of breath and in pain, I got them both onto the driveway. Then a passer-by stopped and helped me, she could see that I was in tears with the pain.

I knew straight away that that I had overdone it and spent most of that day on the bed dosed up with painkillers. Not one of my housemates knew that I was transgender, they all knew I had been in hospital for an operation though, and knew that I was very fragile, so to say I was annoyed at them all for not lending a hand was an understatement. I voiced my opinion to each one as they arrived home that day. I couldn't yet manage to mop the kitchen floor, and that was, by now, in desperate need of a good clean. I was responsible for keeping the communal areas of the house clean, and I woke up the next morning to find the cooker clean and shiny, and the floor had been mopped. It seemed my slightly over-the-top harsh words had got through to at least one of them.

By now I was three more days away from finally saying goodbye to my catheter. I couldn't wait, it was now annoying me so much that I wrote a song about it, a bad one, and I sang it live on Facebook. I went on to sing a couple more songs, my usual karaoke songs.

Lyrics to the 'Catheter song'
Oh catheter, oh catheter
At first you were a superstar allowing me to pee
But as the hours passed and turned to days and days
You dragged me down becoming nothing
But a pain to me
Oh catheter, oh catheter
I hate you so much but know you're saving me
Yes, you're saving me from urinary infection
But catheter my lovely catheter can you
Please just do me one last thing
Oh catheter, oh catheter
Bloody awful catheter can you please just go
Just go now, one more night

> *You'll stop me from sleeping like a baby*
> *And one last time you'll hurt me as the nurse pulls*
> *you away from me*
> *Oh catheter, oh catheter*
> *I'd like to say it's been a blast*
> *But in reality, it's just not true*
> *You've been nothing but a pain in my... Ahem.*
> *Oh, catheter please just fuck off.* (Sing along to your tune.)

I was missing not being able to go and sing out of tune on a Monday night. I had only missed one karaoke night, though; due to the festive holiday season, there hadn't been a karaoke since the 19th of December, and I started thinking in terms of when I could get back to murdering songs via karaoke.

The next karaoke night was the day after my catheter was due to be removed. I had originally planned to return to deafening people with my songs the following week, but I missed it that much that I started to run the idea through my head of going to karaoke that Monday. A big test as to whether I was fit enough to attend karaoke was the monthly LGBT coffee morning. It was the first Saturday of every month, so if could get to that and get through it without any ill-effects, then I might just be able to return to singing again.

For the coffee morning, I still had my catheter, and I would have to drive the car. I devised a plan to attach the drainage bag to my lower leg so I didn't need to go to the toilet, but more importantly, so that I would not potentially be left bursting for the loo whilst possibly stuck in traffic My big fear was wetting myself: I had come close a couple of times when out walking, I could not run and my walking speed was somewhat limited to what most people would call snail's pace.

For the coffee morning, I used duct tape to tape the drainage bag to the inside of my lower left leg I was quite proud of the way I managed to securely attach the bag, and set off by car to the coffee morning, which was about two miles away, four times further than I had driven on my only other drive since the surgery. I made it in relative comfort, which surprised me. It felt invigorating just getting out of the house and chatting to people, almost like my new life was starting from that moment, the moment I rejoined the general population. It was very relaxing and such a boost for me, and I really enjoyed the drive back home too.

That night I had the worst night's sleep yet since my discharge from hospital, partly due to being excited at having the catheter taken out the next day, but mostly due the catheter causing me enough pain to wake me up every time I fell into deep sleep.

My dad arrived early that morning to take me back to hospital. Although I could now drive the car, the twenty-six miles to hospital would have been too much for me. The journey there was not half as bad as the drive home just over two weeks earlier and we arrived a good thirty minutes early.

I was just about to get myself a cappuccino from the drinks machine when I was called by a nurse. In a flash, I had gone from feeling completely fine to feeling very apprehensive. I had heard that catheter removal was painful and although I wanted rid of the horrible thing, I didn't want to experience the procedure. I was back in the same room that I had spent my first hour in prior to surgery and I quickly made myself comfortable on the bed with the television on. I had the same nurse that had dealt with my discharge from hospital after my operation; it was lovely to see her again, and she put me at ease regarding the catheter removal.

I was told to get ready. I stripped from the waist down and

laid on the bed. The nurse came back and deflated the balloon that held the catheter in place. I relaxed as best I could and the nurse then began to slowly pull the catheter out. It was a weird feeling but strangely I felt no pain; it felt almost as though I was having a poo out of my urethra.

Once the catheter was out, I was then on what they call 'TWOC', 'trial without catheter', which meant I had to pee naturally a minimum of three times before they would discharge me. Taking on board plenty of water, it was only an hour before I felt the need to pee, and I placed a cardboard receptacle over the toilet seat, and sat down to pee naturally for the very first time as a 'complete' woman, I had no control over direction, and soaked my bottom, but most of the urine went into the cardboard bowl and was then measured for volume by the nurse.

I found that without the catheter I could now bend over without any pain, I could also sit a little bit more upright too. Two more hours passed and two more toilet visits later, both times soaking my bottom, and the nurse then came back with a machine.

'I just need to do an ultrasound check to see if your bladder is emptying properly.'

'Flipping heck, I'm not pregnant,' I jokingly responded. That made the nurse laugh, so I continued with, 'Mind you, if you do find a heartbeat, medical science will need to be informed.'

'Stop making me laugh, I need a steady hand for this,' the nurse responded. She started to put some jelly-like stuff onto my lower stomach and I shivered. 'Wow, that's cold.'

Just as she placed the monitor onto the jelly material I said, 'Hang on, doesn't it need to be higher up to test for my baby's heartbeat?'

The nurse burst out laughing. 'Honestly, what are you like?' she said while laughing. 'Now don't make me laugh, I need to scan your bladder.'

As she started again, after settling her laughter, I began to make a low sound like a heartbeat and again, she doubled up in fits of laughter, and then I burst into song, 'Papa Don't Preach', the Madonna song about a young girl telling her father that she was pregnant and keeping her baby. Tears from laughing so much were streaming down the nurse's face and she was trying her best to tell me seriously to stop fooling around so that she could get the test done and discharge me. With that I did calm down and the ultrasound showed my bladder to be empty.

Shortly afterwards I got my discharge papers and after a short wait, my friend picked me up from outside the hospital and took me home. As soon as I got home, I began to reclaim my bedroom. I had everything I needed on one side of my bed and I was sleeping on the other side. Now I put everything back on shelves or in cupboards: I wanted the freedom to sprawl out in bed my again.

Going to the toilet was a new experience too. It was like I was learning how to pee all over again; each time I went, I had little or no control over direction, and usually I ended up having to wipe my bottom dry. The area where I'd had surgery less than a month before was still swollen, not massively, just a little bit of swelling, but where the catheter tube had been was still quite swollen and I put my lack of direction and bottom soakings down to that.

Thirty One

Life without a catheter

Being free of the catheter at long last, I was looking forward to finally sleeping right through the night, and being able to spread myself out in my bed. I wasn't ready to give up taking painkillers before bed just yet, and I was looking forward to the day when I could be naked in bed, but I still needed to use sanitary towels, which meant wearing knickers to bed. I was still wearing the larger sizes too, my normal-size knickers were still just a bit too tight due to the swelling.

With me, things never pan out like they should though. Try as I might, I just could not get comfortable in bed and endured a sleepless night. Despite that, I was not in any discomfort, just a dull ache, and decided that if I didn't get any worse, I would try to go to karaoke. The plus side of karaoke was the fact that the hosting pub, the Thomas of York, had a couple of sofas; that meant I would not be faced with either standing up all night, or sitting on a hard bar stool.

All my friends were shocked to see me at karaoke a little

over three weeks after my operation. I wasn't moving very freely, but I could manage a slow walk, and I figured I didn't need my legs to deafen people with my dreadful singing. I always joked on Facebook that people should bring their own earplugs to karaoke ready for when I sing.

It was a great atmosphere. Jane and Wendy, the karaoke hosts, always made it a good night with their banter and interaction with the singers. They had both always been totally supportive of me and what I had achieved during my journey towards being complete, and they surprised me with a present and a card. It was a lovely canvas art, a figure looking into the night sky with shooting stars and the caption, 'Go confidently in the direction of your dreams and live the life you've imagined.' It was perfect and summed me up to a tee.

After an amazing night, full of good singing, and my singing, lots of laughs and yet more wet bums (mine), I went home feeling extremely tired and looking forward to my head greeting the pillow with my eyes firmly shut. An hour later I was awake and rushing to the loo, I had an overwhelming feeling of a full bladder, yet only a trickle came out. Still, my bottom stayed dry for once. Less than thirty minutes later and I was repeating the process with the same result, and so it went on throughout the night. Something was wrong. By my fourth trip to the bathroom, not even a trickle came out and I was getting worried, and I also desperately needed some sleep, but I didn't dare to not go to the bathroom just in case the hoped-for flood came and soaked the bed.

At 5am I was so exhausted through lack of sleep that I took an extra couple of painkillers, stronger ones, that just about knocked me out and I then managed a four-hour sleep. I woke up to a dry bed, which was a relief, but also in need of the bathroom. My joy at soaking my bottom could be measured on the Richter scale. Never had passing urine been so delightful; I didn't care that my bum was dripping wet through, it was just such a huge relief at having an empty bladder.

I never knew what had gone wrong during the night, but I hoped that now that I had opened the floodgates, I would be OK. My next trip to the bathroom was a nervy affair; I was hoping I would be fine, but worried that I would be back to just a trickle and facing the prospect of phoning the hospital with a potential problem. I need not have worried, I soaked my bum again, I was still, in effect, learning how to pee, and hoping the day would soon arrive when I could go to the loo and not have to dry my bottom afterwards.

That afternoon, Tim came to my house so that we could work on our joint presentation for LGBT History Month. We had done the bulk of the presentation a month or so before my surgery, but our presentation date was now just a few weeks away, so we had to work on fine-tuning it and trimming the content down about an hour. We ended up adding more to it, but as we ran through a rehearsal we found that we could present it within our allotted one hour, and settled on a final fine-tuning and rehearsal a few days before we were due to present it to a live audience.

I slept soundly that night, only the third time in recent weeks that I had slept well, so I didn't pin any hopes on now being able to sleep properly again. I put it down to just being so overly tired that I slept through whatever it was that would normally break up my sleep.

After the reasonably hectic few days that had just passed, the next few days saw me getting increasingly bored through a lack of human interaction. People had gone back to work after the holiday season, and I was stuck at home with daytime television back to its usual dreary self. It seemed that my life was two-toned: weekdays were dragging me down with a boredom factor on a par with watching paint dry, and my weekends were filled with people and flew by faster than a rocket.

My first event of the year, and indeed my first whilst recovering from surgery, was the York Pride Drag Race. It was a take on Ru Paul's Drag Race, a great evening's entertainment where the audience, myself included, would vote for our favourite drag act, and the winner would get to perform live on the stage at York Pride later in the year. There were lots of people there that I had not seen for a long time, and it was good catching up with them all. The drag acts were all fantastic, but for me, one stood out head and shoulders above the rest: Tom Tyra. Enough of the audience agreed with me, as Tom won.

I was enjoying life without a catheter. It allowed me to start on the path back towards leading a relatively normal life. I could get out and about, and each day I felt as though I was improving physically. I was now able to discard the sanitary towels and my toilet skills were slowly getting better: sometimes my bottom would remain dry, but not always.

I was now starting to think in terms of a possible return to work maybe a week earlier than planned, but I needed to know how I would cope with a full day being active; I was still only active in short bursts and resting on the bed to recover. The chance to test myself came in late January, just six weeks to the day since my gender reassignment surgery.

It was January 26th and Leeds Gender Clinic had asked me to help them to present a workshop with them for staff at the gender clinic. There were about 150 people there and the day was broken down into smaller workshops on various subjects. The workshop I helped with was on gender, a morning and afternoon workshop to two different audiences. It was an amazing experience and one that I was immensely proud of. It could not have gone any better than it did, and I was so pleased that the gender clinic had even considered me as a person to help them. I knew they had been very impressed with my own transgender workshop, but this was a big step up because I was presenting to an audience of professional clinicians and psychologists.

It was a very long day, but I survived with relatively little pain. I slept very well that night, the start of a run of nights where my sleep looked like it was finally settling down into a normal pattern. By this stage, too, I was no longer needing to take painkillers before going to bed, real progress and I was feeling stronger by the day. I had long held the thought that the catheter had held me back, and this looked to be bearing fruit. I knew I was ahead of schedule with my recovery, and I was now thinking about my return to work, maybe I could start work again even sooner.

Two days after helping the gender clinic with their workshop, I had my own transgender workshop in York. Again, it was packed and the day went extremely well with very positive feedback. For my part, I could give feedback on the surgery to those who were interested in going down that same path. I could give them the finer details of what to expect and maybe one or two things they could do that I failed to do, like ensure I had a good back-up plan if the internet access was down or poor, and how better to relieve the sheer boredom.

I was due back at the hospital for my six-week post-op check-up a few days later. After driving to Leeds from York the previous Thursday, I drove myself to the hospital. As usual, I arrived a good thirty minutes early and had only just got myself a cappuccino when I was called to the consultation room. Mr Church asked a few questions and then inspected his handiwork, my vagina, and he told me he was very pleased with how it was looking and healing. I mentioned that my sick-note would expire the next day and I needed a new one for work, and he asked me how long I felt I would need.

I told Mr Church that I felt another week or so and would be ready to go back to work if it was a phased return on light duties, and so I got the all-clear to resume work on Monday 13th February, a full three weeks ahead of schedule and just fifty-nine days after surgery. I was also given a set of dilators, five in total, from very small to what looked like a small rolling pin.

I had instructions and a DVD and a small bottle of lubrication; I could now start the daily routine of dilating. The purpose, to start with, was to stretch my new vagina, gradually moving up through the sizes until eventually I would be using the largest one. It was a once-a-day routine to last for the first three months, then dropping down over time to just once per week.

By this stage, nerve endings were starting to reconnect; they connected without warning and I would feel a sharp, intense pain for a few seconds before it would ease, but the very first time I dilated, I didn't feel anything. Next day I went into work with my new sick-note and talked through my planned return. I would be doing two weeks of four hours per day, then stepping up an hour per day the following week, and again the week after, and then by week five I would be back to my full-time hours.

The day before my triumphant return to normal work, I had my LGBT History Month presentation. It started with myself and Tim doing our joint presentation on how legislation had changed over the past fifty years since the partial decriminalisation of homosexuality and how 'Prides' had developed over that same period. We had a good audience for a wet and windy Sunday afternoon, and the talk was very well received, with lots of positive feedback. Then it was Tim's turn to talk solo on their specialist subject, being from the black and ethnic minority community and being gay, which was fascinating, and again well received.

Next it was my turn to talk. I spoke about my journey from childhood to present day and being transgender, about how I grew in confidence and dealt with people who used to bully me, through to having surgery and standing there in a room full of people giving a talk less than nine weeks later. I had my audience hanging on every word and fascinated by my life story. I felt a massive glow inside me, the feedback I got blew me away and I went home on cloud nine.

Thirty Two

Returning to work

I wasn't used to waking up to the alarm clock sounding; I hadn't slept at all well, I was nervous yet excited at my impending return to work. I had got my uniform ready the night before such was my excitement; it almost felt like I was starting a brand new job.

I had a good forty-five minutes before I had to leave for work. After checking emails and losing all my lives on Candy Crush, I still had half an hour to spare. I got dressed and kept checking the time before finally leaving the house ten minutes before I needed to. I ended up waiting in my car in the work car park for nearly ten minutes before someone else arrived and for a moment I forgot my code to turn off the alarm to the building.

It didn't take me long to settle in again, and as people arrived for work, they were asking how I was. Soon my manager arrived and I had my return to work interview, before I continued with my light duties. Shortly after the store opened to customers, I was putting some stock on the shelf and let out an involuntary whine as I felt another sharp jabbing pain. A couple of work colleagues thought that I had hurt myself, so I explained that it was my nerve endings connecting.

The day passed quite quickly but by the end of my first shift back, I felt very tired and my feet hurt. I made it through the rest of the week doing my four hours and feeling tired after each shift. By the time I had completed that first week I was very glad to have two days off. My feet were aching and muscles were hurting, but I loved being back at work and it was helping me to build up my strength and take away the boredom I had been suffering.

I had one more week of working four hours per day before I was due to step up by an hour per day each week. After that first week, I was mightily glad that I had one more to build up my strength enough to survive a step up in hours. During that second week at work, I received an email from the Leeds Gender Clinic. They were about to interview people for a new position, psychologist, and I was asked to be part of their interviewing panel. It was an eye-opening day and I learnt so much more about the gender clinic behind the scenes and what's involved, and it made me appreciate them even more.

Each of the candidates were very good in their interviews, but for me, one stood head and shoulders above the others, and each one of the interviewing panel agreed with me. Hercules would be a terrific addition, and would be offered the post.

With my phased return to work going well, despite feeling exhausted after each shift, a sense of normality was returning to my life. For the first time in my life, I could look forward to the rest of my life instead of just looking as far as the surgery. I could start to live and maybe even plan what I hoped might lie ahead for me. Throughout my journey, I had often been asked about one contentious issue: which toilet to use? And it was a question that was not going away.

Over in America, there had been lots of news about the controversial anti-trans bathroom bills, and I had been quite vocal across social media against them. The problem was, America was still quite a staunchly religious country and some states were invoking the Bible in their arguments. They strongly believed that allowing a transgender person to have access to the restroom facilities of the gender opposite to their birth gender would be letting perverts and paedophiles into the same space as women and putting them in great danger.

To Americans, transgender people were men dressing as women and I had a flurry of debates on Twitter with religious Americans as I tried to educate them. I drew on my personal experience of using the men's facilities during the time before I began to transition, and how scared I was in the men's, how I often faced verbal abuse when all I wanted to do was to use the toilet, in comparison to the times when I had waited near the ladies' facilities until I was sure they were empty before entering.

I tried in vain to explain that transgender people were not just people transitioning from male to female, but from female to male too. I did get my point across to a few Americans that forcing transgender people to use the facilities of their birth gender would be putting them at severe risk of verbal abuse or even physical abuse, and that a symbol on a toilet door would not deter someone who was determined, regardless of their gender, pointing out that there had been no cases proven in law of transgender people attacking other people inside restrooms.

Throughout my transition, I always used the ladies' facilities and never encountered any problems, I always felt safer than using the men's, and I had the luxury of UK legislation on my side. I never felt sure which toilets to use before I began to transition when I was out dressed as a woman, but again I had never had any problems in the ladies' but felt constantly in fear in the men's.

Once my phased return to work was complete and I was back to being full-time, it took another couple of weeks before

I would end a shift and not feel like I had run a marathon. I did question whether I had gone back to work a little early, but from returning to work on February 13th, despite almost constantly feeling tired and exhausted, I survived without any problems and by early April I felt that I was back to being fully fit and almost at my pre-surgery levels.

I was now faced with the happy prospect of living my life. It would be quite a few months before I could even think about engaging in any sexual activity, but without testosterone coursing through my body, I didn't feel in any rush to either engage in sexual encounters, or look for romance. I was quite happy being single but now I was open-minded to the possibility of forming a relationship, but I intended to continue fighting the corner of LGBT people worldwide and if love reared its head... I would cross that bridge when I came to it.

I could have been forgiven for resting on my laurels and retreating into a quiet life, but I felt I had a duty to step up my campaigning for other transgender people following in my footsteps and for the gay and lesbian community too. I began to email human rights departments and the United Nations about why I felt they should do more to work with the countries that still had the death penalty as the maximum punishment just for being gay; twelve countries in total from seventy-six worldwide which still made it a criminal offence to be homosexual.

I continued my battle with Americans over their bathroom bills that essentially discriminated against transgender people and put them at risk of serious harm, and I continued working within York to set up what could be considered as safe spaces for transgender people. I was helping and advising people on an individual and group basis and recalling my own memories and drawing on them to show that life does get better if you can get through the hardest part of the transition, the first few years.

My favourite term of endearment that I used was that a transgender person is like a caterpillar: we often see ourselves as ugly in the sense that to be happy, changes must be made. A caterpillar goes into a chrysalis and finally emerges as a beautiful butterfly and a transgender person does the same thing, only their chrysalis is completely invisible and people can see a slow change, before the transgender person eventually gets through virtually every day without any negativity and that's the moment they become the butterfly.

I was now that butterfly in terms of where I was at with my life.

Thirty Three

Stepping into the unknown

On the first anniversary of the transgender workshop, I was back on BBC local radio explaining how it had progressed in its first year, and my hopes for future workshops. It had gone from a local event to other parts of Yorkshire now taking the parts they liked and using them to form their own workshops; my baby was growing.

That first anniversary coincided with a week off work, and I also did a local television show in Bradford, explaining what being transgender meant to me and how I transitioned. It was broadcast to the local Muslim and Asian communities and the feedback from them was one of overwhelming support. I had also been a staunch supporter of diversity and was always quick to defend the minority groups in our country especially considering the apparent rise in racism that occurred after the EU referendum and subsequent terrorist attacks in London and Manchester.

As I have always tried to explain during some of my talks, in all walks of life, in all groups and religions, there are and always will be a tiny minority with extreme views which may sometimes spill over into violent acts and acts of terror.

My world was flipped on its head, I had just about recovered from Leeds Pride hot on the heels of a night out in Manchester, and I got a text message from work, saying could I give them a call. The resulting phone call was not worrying: I needed to go into work for a meeting. I just assumed it was a management meeting, possibly about Christmas and the upcoming major layout changes to the store to trade Christmas stock, which were usually planned in early August.

That meeting turned out to a one-to-one meeting in which the manager read a statement about the impact of 'Brexit' and the fall of the pound against other currencies and how the company were now entering into negotiations about a management restructure and my job was one of those 'at risk'. I left that meeting feeling numb. I could ill afford to lose my job; transgender people like myself find it incredibly hard to find work. For the first time since my surgery I felt downbeat. The official consultation process began, and it was confirmed that my job role was being removed. I had options: I could drop down to level 1 and lose £2 per hour. Over a thirty-five-hour week that equated to £300 per month, in retail that was far too much money for me to lose per month. The other two options I had were to either take redundancy, worth about £5,000 for ten years' service, or I could apply for the new team leader role, basically the same role I was in, but with more responsibility, different working hours and no extra pay.

It was an easy choice for me, I applied for what I saw as my own job, just under a new title, but I had strong reservations about aspects of the role, which I voiced. I wanted clarity on the new shift patterns: would I be working late evening and how often? Would I be able to test those new shift patterns before making a final decision? Would the evening supervisor be doing work as opposed to going missing when the going got tough? Would I get fully trained on the new responsibilities? Would I still be able to take redundancy if it didn't work out how I expected?

Not one of those questions were answered in a positive way. I got no clarity other than saying that, should I be successful at the interview for the team leader position, and accepted the post, I would have a thirteen-week trial period during which I would be fully trained, new shifts would be trialled and the opportunity to take redundancy would still be in place until the thirteen-week period was completed.

The day of my interview arrived, the alarm clock sounded but I couldn't reach it. I had spent most of the night in absolute agony and not slept, I had finally drifted off to sleep an hour before the alarm was due to sound, dosed up on painkillers. I still couldn't move far enough to reach the alarm clock without my back going into spasms. Quarter of an hour passed before the alarm stopped, but there was no way I could make it to work, let alone attend my interview. My world was collapsing around me and I felt powerless to stop it. I was in tears as I phoned work and said I would not be in due to my back. I knew I was going miss my interview and lose my chance to keep my job.

After drifting in and out of sleep, I phoned my GP and made an appointment for that afternoon. Within an hour I phoned them back to cancel and request a home visit: I couldn't walk, never mind drive the car to the surgery. My GP left me with seven days' supply of extremely powerful painkillers and a diagnosis of a trapped nerve causing muscle spasms, so I informed work that I would be off for the rest of that week at least.

I had daily text messages from my manager wanting to know when I could return to work to have my interview, but the medication I was on was causing me to hallucinate for twenty minutes or so after taking it; this was usually followed by a good sleep and only then was I getting two or three hours relatively pain-free before the next dose would be due. I couldn't give my manager a time when I would be able to travel to work, have my interview and get home before the pain became so bad that I would need my medication again. I certainly couldn't risk driving straight after taking my painkillers: if I got stuck in traffic or delayed and did not make the sanctuary of the work car park before the hallucinations began, I would cause an accident. But waiting until after the 'induced' sleep wouldn't give me a realistic window to get to work, be interviewed, and travel home before it became too painful to drive.

The deadline day for interviews arrived and I was on the brink of losing my job. My manager phoned yet again, and again I had to say that I could not travel. He gave me a choice, he could come to my home and interview me, or it could be done over the phone. All my preparation and notes were in my locker at work, but I decided at that point that I had everything to gain and nothing to lose; I was out of a job if I didn't do the interview, so I decided on the telephone option.

Thirty minutes later the phone rang, and it was interview time. I struggled through the questions, remembering what I could from my prep work and finding it very hard to think clearly. At times there were long pauses as I tried to manage my pain, but after about an hour or so of questions, the interview ended. I had messed it up, deep down I knew I had not done myself justice with some of my answers and I just lay there and cried. Why did life always find a way to kick me when life started to look good?

My back was starting to ease slightly. It could have been the medication, or it could have been on the mend, but I now had just over a week to recover enough to be able to carry out my social obligations. I was due to go to Beninbrough Hall for a project that had been planned since February; a lot of media had been released in the run-up to the October event, and my place in that event was now in jeopardy.

The day after my telephone interview, I got the call from work to inform me that I had passed the interview, with ease as it happened, but I had passed and on my return to work I would be formally offered my job. I raised my concerns about aspects of the new role, and of the evening supervisor; I made it clear that some things had to change and I was quite prepared to walk away if they didn't.

My back was steadily improving too, and I began to target a return to work. The hallucinations from the painkillers weren't lasting as long either, which was a relief as I didn't like seeing dinosaurs coming towards me and snakes wrapping themselves around my arms. In hindsight, I should have contacted my GP about the hallucinations.

The following week I was back at work, albeit on light duties. I was formally offered the role of team supervisor, which in effect was my old role, but with added responsibility and duties. I had secured my future and could now look forward to the following weekend which would see me taking my place in the seat occupied by David Hoyle a year earlier.

Following on from 'Portraits Untold', Beninbrough Hall were doing a follow up called 'Sitters and their Stories' with Tanya Raabe-Webber again the artist. I had been asked to be the sitter back in February, and in partnership with Beninbrough Hall, I had also been asked to do a joint presentation with Beninbrough Hall at the National Trust's annual conference which they called a 'Convestival', a cross between a conference and a festival. That had taken place in June and was an amazing couple of days listening to presentations and talks and of course delivering my talk as part of Beninbrough Hall's presentation. Now, I was back at Beninbrough Hall for a day of being grilled by an audience whilst having my portrait painted.

It was a very surreal moment taking my place in front of an audience who were about to ask questions about my life and draw pictures of me. It was even more surreal having Tanya Raabe-Webber painting me and projecting audience members' drawings of me onto the canvas alongside her own painting of me. I took a leaf out of David Hoyle's book and changed outfits at the interval; for the first session I was quite casual in jeans, trainers and purple top, but for the remaining two sessions I was in my Pride outfit, a rainbow-coloured dress with a rainbow sequin hat, rainbow tights, pink shoes and to top it off, I drew a rainbow flag on my cheek.

The questions came thick and fast and it was very enlightening knowing that people of all ages were gaining a knowledge of transgender people and drawing my portrait into the bargain. I felt truly humbled to be part of the project and very honoured to be taking David Hoyle's place. My portrait was to be finished properly at Tanya's studio, just like she had done with David Hoyle's twelve months earlier, and then it would return to Beninbrough Hall in early spring of 2018, where it was due to be on show to visitors as part of their 'Making her Mark – Creative Women' exhibition. Eventually I would be presented with the portrait, but I couldn't wait to see 'Lisa's Freedom' – the name given to the portrait – hanging in pride of place at Beninbrough Hall.

Back at work, my future was secure, but something wasn't sitting very well with me. I wasn't convinced that anything would be done towards getting the evening supervisor to be more of a team player and work alongside the people she would be supervising. I was worried about the new shift patterns as we had no information on how they would work, and also worried about the impact the evening supervisor would have on my morning team once we began to 'share' each other's teams. I voiced my concerns again, and stressed that I needed to be able to try out the new shift patterns before making a final decision on my own future. I had a thirteen-week period to decide, as did the company, and I could still opt for redundancy during that period.

It was now the peak trading time for retail, the run-up to Christmas, and the deliveries from head office were bigger than we'd ever had before. It became a daily routine to walk in at 6am and finish working the delivery from the previous night, that meant that we were not moving the warehouse stock onto the shelves, and the warehouse very quickly reached breaking point. We had never cancelled a delivery in my ten years at the store, but during November and early December, we cancelled seven. I couldn't help thinking that if the evening supervisor pulled her weight, her team would get through more of the delivery and we would stand a chance of not having to cancel any deliveries.

I and a couple of others had done a week of nights, and seen again first hand just how much, rather, how little, the evening supervisor did. There were a couple of small deliveries that didn't get close to being completed; her team were not exactly trying and who could blame them when their supervisor was missing for extended periods? It was demoralising knowing we had to put our tasks on hold to finish off a delivery that should have been completed with ease.

Back to working my regular mornings, I began seriously to consider my future. Customers year-on-year were becoming ever ruder, just a small percentage, but it was those who were affecting my moods more than the majority who were happy that we'd given them good customer service. One particular day stood out, it was very busy and quite stressful. 'Where are your glasses?' I had my back to the person, and so not knowing who the comment was directed towards and assuming it was a conversation between two customers, I continued to place stock onto the shelf. 'Oy! I asked where your glasses are?' I turned around to see a customer looking a little put out that I had ignored him the first time, 'Oh, sorry, I didn't realise you were talking to me,' I replied, 'if you would like to follow me I'll show you.'

I took the man to the kitchen section where we kept the wine glasses, shot glasses, pint glasses and mixer glasses, thinking being close to Christmas he wanted glasses for the party season.

'Not these glasses, reading glasses, you fucking idiot!' he snarled.

'You didn't say reading glasses and it is party season, reading glasses are over there,' I said, pointing near the tills, and I walked away. I was fuming, there was no need for that language and deep inside I wanted to tell him he should try going to Specsavers, but that could have got me in trouble, so I bit my tongue instead.

Soon after that I answered a phone call from a customer 'Have you got any 100-watt lightbulbs?'

'I'm sure we'll have something close to that, the old-style bulbs are discontinued, they are all energy savers now, so it'd be the closest to 100-watt that you'd need,' I answered.

'No, it must be 100-watt, and how much are they?' asked the customer.

'The old-style bulbs were outlawed by the EU, nobody sells them anymore, the modern-style energy savers are lower wattage but give a similar output to the old bulbs. We don't have any that give an equivalent to exactly 100-watts, the closest would be something around 20-watts in energy-saver bulbs with an output equivalent to around 97-watts in old terms,' I said.

'I just want one that is 100-watts, is that too hard for you to understand?' the woman on the phone retorted.

'They don't come in 100-watts anymore,' but before I could explain I was interrupted.

'What kind of bloody idiot are you? Of course they do! I have one in my hand,' the woman was getting angry now.

'There really is no need to insult me, I am trying to explain that type of bulb you have now is no longer manufactured.' Again, I was interrupted.

'When I talk to a tranny I'll use whatever language I like, put me through to someone with a brain.' My telephone voice always appeared to give me away.

At that point I just put the phone down, I was stressed because of the workload and customers like that were not helping. I decided it was time I took my tea break and started to make my way from the till area towards the warehouse, but a customer asked for help while I was en route.

'Excuse me, where do you keep beruca?' asked the elderly gent.

'Erm, what is it?' I replied.

'It's that thing you put in water and it goes orange,' he responded.

'Oh, I've never heard of it, we do have Robinson's orange juice if that's any good?' I asked.

'Are you stupid? It's a vitamin you put into water,' he snapped back.

'Ah, you mean Berocca! It's over there somewhere, I'm too stupid to take you though,' I responded, and walked away.

As we approached the middle of December, I was growing increasingly frustrated at work. We still hadn't trialled any new shift patterns and after a week off, using holidays, I was flooded with complaints from my morning team about the evening supervisor who had covered my week off as part of her training for the new roles we were moving into. Every complaint was along the same lines, that she was lazy and went missing for long periods. This just added to my belief that working alongside her again would be impossible for me.

The whole situation was getting me down, I was no longer enjoying my work, but I had that carrot dangling in front of me, the opportunity to take redundancy. Deciding to keep all my available options open whilst I thought long and hard about my future, I began to look at job vacancies online and saw one that stood out, which involved working for the civil service.

Back in October I had gone to a top security prison and given a talk to a group of inmates, part of the prison's LGBT group and some other inmates who had an interest. I was intrigued as to how LGBT people in the prison system coped with life and hoped my talk went some way towards educating the non-LGBT inmates and helping the LGBT inmates. It had gone down very well, and I was asked by the officer who had arranged my talk if I would consider going back at various intervals and delivering more talks. Of course, I jumped at that chance, but the final decision would be down to the prison and their available funding, they weren't willing to let me do it without some form of payment, so I just had to wait and see what, if anything, came of the idea.

I applied for the vacancy in the civil service, and gave serious thought to how my next few weeks would pan out. The option of taking redundancy was still there, but it was now the week before Christmas and in a further four weeks the option of redundancy would no longer be on the table. The first thing that I had to decide was whether I stayed in my current workplace; could I continue indefinitely getting up each day and not looking forward to going to work? Was the situation likely to improve with regards to the evening supervisor? Would the new shift patterns suit my lifestyle?

The first two questions were answered with a resounding 'No.' I was not prepared to allow my job to drag me down into depression, and I could not see any prospect of my manager doing anything about the evening supervisor, and I couldn't answer the third question because I had not had the chance to trial the new shift patterns; we had no idea of how those shift patterns would look, as no draft rotas had been done.

The next thing I needed to decide was, could I take redundancy without having a new job? And how long could I survive without a new job? Well, I could leave regardless of my job situation, though it would be a massive risk to take if I had no new job to walk into. I could survive about three months without any income coming in other than what the benefit system paid, but if I only managed to find something that was part-time, it would allow me to stretch my redundancy to six to eight months before I would be in financial trouble, and lots of places in and around York were constantly asking for new part-time staff.

It was a conundrum; it didn't want to make a rash decision and regret it, but just before Christmas I had a bit of do with another member of staff that resulted in me lowering my halo and telling her to 'do what the fuck you want'. It was on the shop floor while we had customers in, it was very unprofessional of me and if that member of staff had chosen to report it, I could have been in serious trouble, it was gross misconduct.

A nervous weekend passed, the Monday before Christmas Day came and went and there was no mention of my 'incident'. It looked like it had gone unreported and I had escaped the possible sack, my mood lifted a little and I was starting to err on the side of not taking a risk with my future, but just to compound matters, I was offered an interview for the civil service vacancy, on January 12th.

The next day I was called to the manager's office, nothing unusual in that, I assumed it would be to go through the workload for the final few days Christmas sales and changing the store layout from Christmas focussed to January sale. I was greeted with the manager and assistant manager sat at the manager's desk and an empty chair for myself. It was a formal meeting: I was in trouble.

I was informed what the complaint was, and what I was 'alleged' to have said and was asked to give my version of events. I told the truth, I held my hands up and said that I had used the 'F' word albeit there were no witnesses around and that I had instantly regretted lowering my halo. Had I denied it, I would have been suspended on pay while an investigation took place, and then I would have had a disciplinary meeting at which I could potentially have been dismissed. The fact that I admitted what I had said, and regretted it, saved my bacon. I was given a letter of concern about my conduct.

I'd lowered my colours once, given my frustrations at work, and I feared it could it easily happen again. That day, I made my mind up to take redundancy, but I didn't rush home and type out my letter requesting it. I decided I would get Christmas out of the way, and present my letter on Boxing Day.

I got through that week and the more I thought about things, the more I thought that it was a knee-jerk reaction, and I decided to think long hard, and use my days off, New Year's Eve and New Year's Day, to decide once and for all what I would do.

On January 1st I printed my letter requesting my redundancy giving just over one week's notice. Tears were streaming down my face as I slid it into the envelope ready for the next morning. I was about to end ten years of service and my final day would be January 13th. I had no job to walk into, and I knew I was taking a huge risk. I did have the comfort of knowing I had an interview for the civil service the day before the curtain would be due to fall on my current job.

I had an uneasy sleep that night, and felt quite nervous at work as I set my morning team off on their jobs. Before starting my own jobs, I popped my letter on the manager's desk and instantly felt some relief. I couldn't explain why, I just felt like a weight had suddenly been lifted off my shoulders. The manager was unexpectedly calm about it, he told me he understood my reasons for going and although disappointed, he respected my decision. He did ask a few times over the following days if I would reconsider, but my mind was made up. I was dreading that final week, I had so many memories and friends that I would be saying goodbye to. Each time I thought about how my final week would pan out, I welled up with tears.

My final week was emotional to say the least. Each day there was someone whom I would not see again before my final shift, and each day I cried. I was crying because I was walking out on ten years of my life and stepping into the unknown. I had no job; the job sites I was checking daily were full of retail jobs and very little else, and I wanted to escape retail completely. The changing attitudes of customers had been a factor in my decision, a small one, but a factor nevertheless.

All my eggs were firmly in one basket: the civil service job. On the morning of my interview, I had a half-day safeguarding adults course to attend as part of my role within York LGBT Forum. It took my mind off worrying about the interview, and from that course I went home, had a quick change of clothes and drove to the interview. I should have been nervous with what seemed like my whole future resting on the next forty-five minutes, but I was calm. Maybe it was all the talks I had given to varying audiences, or maybe I just had such a good feeling about things, but I was calm. I sailed through the interview and came out thinking I done very well. I was quietly confident, but I had a week to wait before I would know anything.

The next day was the final day at work. I was down for a full day looking after the tills, normally I would just open the store and watch over the first hour or so of trade, but I was glad I had a full shift on tills as it was a Saturday and it would keep me busy and my mind occupied. At varying intervals during that final shift, the tears rolled down my face as other people finished their shift and said their goodbyes to me. I was presented with numerous cards and gifts as one-by-one people finished work. I still had the hardest goodbye of all to come though.

Sarah had been the person I confided in about my transition; she had remained my best friend at work, and was sorry that I was leaving. She was due to start her shift as I finished mine. She had been there for me every time I needed a shoulder to lean on, or someone to just listen to me, when I had to let my emotions fly.

As I finished my shift I did a quick tour of the shop saying goodbye to people. Lord knows what the customers must have thought, but before I made it to the sanctuary of the warehouse, the tears were streaming down my face. I composed myself as best as I could and made my way to the staff canteen, and Sarah. I was never going to leave to building without more tears flowing, just one look at Sarah and the tears came flooding out again. She had got me a beautiful leaving gift, a figurine called 'The journey'. It summed me up perfectly. It was heart-wrenching to leave after ten years, the highs had been awesome, the laughs had been side-splitting and they made up for the lows, and it was fitting that Sarah signed me out of building to bring down the curtain on my career in retail. It was the end of an era.

I have no idea how I drove home with the tears still streaming down my cheeks, but once home, the reality of not putting on that red uniform again started to sink in. As I laid out all the cards and gifts to take a photo, it dawned on me for the first time just how much I had touched the lives of my now former work colleagues. Between them, they must have spent a small fortune on me and I got a lump in throat just thinking about how much I would miss them.

Later that day, I did a live Facebook post dedicated to everyone I had worked with, and because I knew nobody would step up and take over singing silly songs and making people laugh at work, I sang as a farewell to them. Probably for the first time ever, I was almost in tune; holding back my tears and trying my best to keep my emotions in check, I blasted out Frank Sinatra's 'My Way'.

The next few days passed by rather mundanely then, on the Wednesday, with all my general household chores done, I found myself wondering what to do with my time. I was fed up of looking at endless retail vacancies, and I was bored. My mind was wandering, and I was missing work; for the first time I was beginning to think that I had made a massive mistake, that I was staring at a bleak future where a return to retail would be forced on me by the job centre.

Next day an email arrived from the Ministry of Justice job site. I stared at the unopened email for a good ten minutes, too scared to open it, then I had a phone call which distracted me, and I decided to have breakfast before checking the email; I couldn't face bad news on an empty stomach. It was over an hour before I nervously clicked on the email to open it. The opening line of that email was…

Dear Lisa,

Thank you for attending your recent interview/assessment. I am pleased to make you a conditional offer of employment, subject to your successful completion of pre-employment checks, which include the completion of a health questionnaire.

The tears came instantly, tears of joy, I was going to be working for the Civil Service. The job offer was subject to various checks, but I had never been in trouble with the law and certainly wasn't a terrorist, so that just left being able to prove that I was legally entitled to work in the UK. My birth certificate still had 'male' as my sex, but I had informed them at the interview that I had changed my gender, I just had not yet applied for a gender recognition certificate because I was waiting for the Government review of the 2004 Gender Recognition Act to be done. All I had to do was supply various paperwork and wait for the checks to be completed, which I was told would take up to twelve weeks.

After taking a huge risk and stepping into the unknown, I had come up smelling of roses and the next chapter of my life was about to begin.